EFFECTIVE MANAGEMENT
of MENTAL ILLNESS
WITHOUT WIDENING RECIDIVISM
In CONTEMPORARY CORRECTIONAL SETTING

EFFECTIVE MANAGEMENT *of* MENTAL ILLNESS WITHOUT WIDENING RECIDIVISM *In* CONTEMPORARY CORRECTIONAL SETTING

(A Review of IDOC Treatment Centers& Supervisory Training Memos)

Stephen B. Oladipo, PhD

To order additional copies of this book, contact:
Xlibris
844-714-8691
www.Xlibris.com
Orders@Xlibris.com
844373

CONTENTS

List of Tables and Charts

Dedication

To God and only true God; without whom,
this whole journey will be dead end.

Philosophy of Reckoning

Destination is destination; every stone-thrown
in the journey of destination is designed
to add to the contours of destiny.

Time reveals what we go through; we
decide how we go through it.

Fate is neither friend nor enemy; it's just
acting its path in the way of providence.

Acknowledgement is a debt, the same is recompense.
To everyone who has enhanced my experience in
the pathway of career progression, I acknowledge
you. This mile-stone of a study would not have
been made possible without your contributions.

List of Acronyms

AD: Administrative Directive
ACLU: America Civil Liberties Union
BHT: Behavioral Health Therapist
BMU: Behavioral Modification Unit
BOP: Bureau of Prison
BOJ: Bureau of Justice
CAO: Chief Administrative Officer
CTO: Corrections Treatment Officer
CTOS: Corrections Treatment Officer Supervisor
CTSSS: Corrections Treatment Senior Security Supervisor
DAO: Duty Administrative Officer
DR: Departmental Rule
ETC: Elgin Treatment Center
ERT: Emergency Response Team
FBP: Federal Bureau of Prison
ID: Institutional Directives
IDOC: Illinois Department of Corrections
JITC: Joliet Inpatient Treatment Center
JTC: Joliet Treatment Center
MH: Mental Health

MI: Mentally Ill
MHP: Mental Health Practitioner
NIJ: National Institute of Justice
QMHP: Qualified Mental Health Professional
RN: Registered Nurse
SMI: Seriously Mentally Ill
SOP: Standard Operating Procedure
US: United States
WHO: World Health Organization

Definition of Terms

Note: To enhance understanding, the words and phrases described in this book have the following meanings designated to them:

(i) **Court Agreement**: An agreement between two or more parties, concluded or documented in a record, that designates a court for the purpose of deciding disputes that have arisen or may arise in connection with a particular legal relationship.

(ii) **Court Injunction**: Means an order issued by a judge that forces a person or entity to perform an action or stop taking certain action.

(iii) **Committed person**: Means a person committed to the Department of corrections, he or she cannot be an employee of the Department. A committed person has also been described within the contents as an offender, a resident, a patient and as an individual-in-custody. These words or designations have been interchangeably used in this book to describe the same (committed) person.

(iv) **Correctional institution or facility**: Means any building or part of a building where individuals-in-custody are kept in a secured manner.

(v) **Discipline**: Rules and regulations for the maintenance of order.

(vi) **Individuals-in-Custody**: It is the less aggressive title accorded offenders or inmates who are currently serving terms with Illinois Department of Corrections.

(vii) **Offender**: Will be regarded as a person committed to the Department of corrections or to the custody of the Department.

(viii) **Patient**: This title is also interchangeably used to describe an offender or an inmate under care in Joliet Treatment Centre and Elgin Treatment Centre, Illinois.

(ix) **Recidivism**: Recidivism, in the context of this book, can be defined as re-offence, which results in re-arrest, reconviction and return to incarceration. That is a relapse into criminal behavior after receiving sanctions or undergone intervention for a previous crime.

(x) **Resident**: This is the title which an offender or inmate under residential Mental Health treatment in Joliet Treatment Centre go by.

(xi) **Seriously Mentally Ill**: Refers to an offender who is diagnosed as being mentally ill "as a result of a mental disorder as defined in the current edition of the Diagnostic and Statistical Manual of Mental

Disorders (DSM) of the American Psychiatric Association, exhibits impaired emotional, cognitive or behavioral functioning that interferes seriously with his or her ability to function adequately except with supportive treatment or services. These individuals also must either currently have, or have had within the past year, a diagnosed mental disorder, or must currently exhibit significant signs and symptoms of a mental disorder. A diagnosis of alcoholism or drug addiction, of developmental disorders, or of any form of sexual disorder shall not, by itself, render an individual seriously mentally ill. The combination of either a diagnosis or significant signs and symptoms of a mental disorder and an impaired level of functioning, as outlined in this definition, is necessary for one to be considered seriously mentally ill. Whether a person meets the criteria of seriously mentally ill is initially determined by a comprehensive, professional clinical assessment conducted by a Department Mental Health Professional in order to determine if the individual has a diagnosable mental disorder as defined by the current DSM and to establish the person's overall level of functioning. The appropriate threshold to establish level of functioning that equates to a serious mental illness includes serious impairments in capacity to recognize reality in work, school or learning environments; frequent problems with the authority/rules; occasional combative behavior;

serious impairments in relationships with friends and family; serious impairments in judgment, thinking and mood; and serious impairment due to anxiety. These disturbances must be observed in at least one of the listed areas." (Ill. Admin. Code tit. 20 § 504.12).

(xii) **Victim**: The person who suffers the effects of a crime committed

Foreword

Despite all challenges, it is pertinent to bring to the fore of attention that, Pablo Stewart, MD (2017) did state in the concluding paragraph of his 133 pages Federal Monitoring report that: "IDOC has considerably improved the quality of the mental health services offered to the offender population during the first year of the settlement. Areas of improvement included as listed: providing timely screening and mental health evaluations in the R&C units; transfer of seriously mentally ill offenders from facility to facility; a significant reduction of segregation time for mentally ill offenders; implementation of offender orientation procedures at all IDOC facilities; the proper use of physical restraints for mental health purposes; and structured and unstructured activities being offered at the two operating RTUs and certain segregation units."

The above does not however change the narrative that the department has contended with the challenges of mental Illness issues among the offenders within its confine for decades without specialized resources to explore the scope with its traditional responsibilities. There was no clear-cut, structural or resource-enhanced institutionalized programming to astutely address the growing concern within the correctional system over the period. In 2016 however, the mounting pressure for status-recognition from an evolving group of individuals-in-custody eventually orchestrated the game-changing class-action litigation. Incumbent upon this lawsuit documented as: "Rasho v Baldwin," the emanating injunction was in favor of the plaintiff against the state of Illinois and the Department of Corrections. Consequently, there is currently a mental health status-recognition for certain individuals-in-custody serving under Illinois Department of Corrections as of today. This status recognition interprets to mean deployment of specialized programming and treatment. It also interprets to mean a new phase in correctional setting. Nonetheless, Illinois Department of Corrections (IDOC) became one of the foremost departments of corrections to distinctly establish an institution/facility where greater percentage of correctional programming will directly focus on mental health treatments. The just completed multimillion-dollar state-of-the-art in-patient hospital in Joliet, Illinois further demonstrated the political will of the state's authority in swift response to managing this problem.

In reviewing the enormous responsibility which mental health developmental issues pose within the correctional setting however, it becomes necessary to highlight key areas of challenges overtime. These areas have included: (i) Identification of individual-related symptoms and behavioral expectations, which often vary from patient(s) to patient(s). (ii) Deployment of specific/individualized mental health programming vis-à-vis ideal programming duration for this growing population of Individuals-in-Custody (iii) The straining supply-pull of expert-professionals to conduct required programs. (iv) The slowness in success-rate in treating behavioral-related SMI "Patients" (v) Grouping challenge(s): where protocol advocates customized grouping of same-level of programming-need patients; the behavioral-related Patients are taking advantage of this grouping approach to create negative peer-influence synergy and harnessing the group-effort against institutional regulations to cause collusion and complicate the treatment process (vi) Addiction to particular psychotropic medication is altogether another issue within the treatment process (vii) The rate of "Patients" recycling system between facility to facility to curtail staff burn-out as against programming focus has been criticized (viii) The growing percentage of 'individuals-in-custody" awaiting mental health treatment across various correctional facilities vis-à-vis resource-availability is also a concern. (ix) Individuals-in-custody's willingness-question to participate in the treatment process versus continuous disruptive behavioral display after enlistment. (x) "Patients" restrictions for safety purposes versus the goal of programming and/or purpose of enlistment. (xi) Another challenge is found in the ability to be able to conduct the traditional duties of corrections while attempting to comprehend patients' 'individualistic demeanor' versus same patients' mental health behavioral issues, without compromising the understanding that such patients are term-serving individuals-in-custody. These issues (Mental Illness concerns) and more, further impeded the process of 'justice' where victims of crime are on the sideline relying on the ability of the state and its institutions to serve justice.

Following the above, it is obvious managing mental illness related concerns with traditional approach is in adequate. Nonetheless, the success of the new initiative must be multi-dimensional. It should engender views and incorporate inputs from relevant sphere of endeavors (multi-disciplinary), knowing that programming to treat mental illness issues in a penitentiary jurisdiction would require a combo-effort to treating the embedded propensity to committing crime in the individual(s) as well. Addressing this propensity to committing crime has been the primary focus of correction through offenders' rehabilitation. The tools it offers and the alternative means the system provides these individuals through the process of conditioning and adaptation to protocols within its setting. This adaptation procedure scours away unruly tendency overtime. This underscores the challenge of interference between treating mental illness and the correctional need to remedy criminalistic tendencies. This importance is crystallized in situation where repeated scenarios are pointers to the reality that some incarcerated individuals will milk the process of treatment without implementation of holistic approach. Without doubt, an asymmetric approach to mental illness treatment within the correctional setting will most likely leave the process of correction more susceptible to ineffectiveness (recidivism), especially, where focus to addressing mental illness takes preference and criminalistic symptoms become latent concern. This is the more reason participatory review of treatment measures by all stakeholders within the criminal justice system is imperative. This review equally becomes critical in view of incessant court-injunctions which continue to advance restrictions to tightening both correctional and psychiatrists' control measures. This is where the judicial verdicts must be conscious of the greater risks of creating a vulnerable correctional setting in a bid to accommodate individualized mental health situations. More so, it is important to understand that the job of creating a safe society is everybody's business, starting with the provision of the law and the interpretation of it. The judicial institution therefore needs to be wary of "sentencing advantages" to lowering correctional procedural expectations geared towards effective re-entrance of offenders back into the society. Again, this advocacy becomes imperative to checkmate the noted surge in the rate of recidivism among offenders identified with Mental Health issues in recent time.

Realistically, with the sustained self-harming behaviors that have mostly locked many SMI offenders to live under pleasurable treatments within the 5-star hospitals around the cities, the reason for the recent surge in recidivism among SMI offenders could be fathomed. This is where conscious effort is required to balance accommodation with the overall process of serving justice. Having the understanding that encouraging bad behaviors, in any form, will increase the 'pool' of victims of crime, since there will be no 're-offender' (recidivism) without a crime being committed. In reality, most crime committed leaves the larger society with more victims of crime. Meanwhile, the larger percentages of these victims of crime are mostly the law-abiding citizens. These are usually men and women who are going about their daily businesses and/or just caring for their families. This list of victims can involve anyone and everyone within the society, both high and low; rich or poor; anybody can be a victim. Additionally, recidivism also keeps pressure on state budgeting and expenditure, aside blocking treatment opportunities for 'genuine offenders' in demand of sincere correctional treatments.

Hence, there is a need for resurgence and enhanced proactiveness. The state architecture must rally support for continued formation of bylaws and institutional provisions to assist the process with judicial proceedings, law-enforcement and correctional institutions' improved effectiveness. That is, the effectiveness that lies in the institution's ability to serve justice in a correctional approach manner especially in view of mental health and issues associated with it. Knowing for certain that, the mission is to guarantee successful community reentries without compromising the safety and security of the civil populace and/or normal citizens.

Chapter One

1.0 Introduction

According to U.S. Department of Justice (2006), at "midyear 2005 more than half of all prison and jail inmates had a mental health problem, including 705,600 inmates in State prisons, 78,800 in Federal prisons, and 479,900 in local jails. These estimates represented 56% of State prisoners, 45% of Federal prisoners, and 64% of jail inmates. The findings in this report were based on data from personal interviews with State and Federal prisoners in 2004 and local jail inmates in 2002." The National Commission on Correctional Health Care reported the following prevalence estimates of mental illness within State prisons: "between 2.3 and 3.9 percent of inmates are estimated to have schizophrenia or another psychotic disorder, 13.1 to 18.6 percent have major depression, and between 2.1 and 4.3 percent have bipolar disorder" (Human Right Watch, 2012). Sirotich (2009) furthered on this when he stated that, research conducted in the United States found that between 28 and 52 percent of those with SMI have been arrested at least once. "Overall, offenders with mental illness have higher rates of recidivism when compared with offenders without mental illness,' says Lovell, Gagliardi & Peterson, (2002). Cloyes et al., (2010) corroborated this assertion, stating: "One study reported that 64 percent of offenders who were mentally ill were rearrested within 18 months of release, compared with 60 percent of offenders without mental illness."

Reanalyzing the above in more succinctly scenario, sharing knowledge of occurrence will aid better understanding. One of such incidents like related others, during most staff responses to many episodes of self-harming within the correctional treatment centers, the first statement from most individuals-in-custody classified as Seriously Mentally Ill has remained: "Take me to outside Hospital!" To enrich this knowledge further, one of the mentally ill individual-in-custody had once stated, as quoted: "I have 3 more months left here (in prison) with various inconclusive surgeries, how do you guys want me to survive if I get out this place?" This is one question among many, which sets the pace for the timeliness of this study. This is why every opinionist, and/or interest group outside of correctional institution who believes adopting an asymmetric approach in the treatment of mentally ill offenders is the ideal must also ponder on the effects of the above statement as it relatives to recidivism and overall safety of the larger society.

Indiana Department of Correction in its Recidivism reports for year 2020 defines recidivism as a return to incarceration within three years of the offender's date of release from a state correctional institution. According to National Institute of Justice (2018), recidivism refers to a person's relapse into criminal behavior, often after the person receives sanctions or undergoes intervention for a previous crime. This Bureau of Justice's statistical studies found high rates of recidivism among released prisoners. Examining the recidivism patterns of former prisoners during a 9-year follow-up period in Alpher, Durose & Markman, (2018) analysis, the researchers found that: (i) the 401,288 state prisoners released in 2005 had 1,994,000 arrests during the 9-year period, an average of 5 arrests per released prisoner. Sixty percent (60%) of these arrests occurred during the first four (4) years through to nine (9) years of release. (ii) an estimated 68% of released prisoners were arrested within 3 years, 79% within 6 years, and 83% within 9 years. (iii) eighty-two (82%) percent of prisoners arrested during the 9-year period were arrested within the first 3 years. (iv) almost half (47%) of prisoners who did not have an arrest within 3 years of release were arrested during the fourth (4th) to ninth (9th) year of release. (v) forty-five percent (45%) of released prisoners were arrested during the first (1st) year following their release, while twenty-four (24%) were arrested within the years under the ninth (9th) year of study.

Benecchi (2021) stated: "Recidivism clogs the criminal justice system." In their contributions to recidivism concerns also, McKean and Ransford (2004) of center for impact research stated: "Rates of recidivism reflect the degree to which released inmates have been rehabilitated and the role correctional programs (strategies) play in reintegrating prisoners into society. The rate of recidivism in the U.S. is estimated to be about two-thirds (2/3), which means that two-thirds (2/3) of released inmates will be re-incarcerated within three years. High rates of recidivism result in tremendous costs both in terms of public safety and in tax dollars spent to arrest, prosecute, and incarcerate reoffenders. High rates of recidivism also lead to devastating social costs to the communities…"

With continuous depletion of family institution in the United States therefore, depression is a concern. Other mental health issues, such as psychotic disorders, mania, anxiety and so on, threaten the wellbeing of offenders when correction centers become the repositories for young males and females within the western hemisphere. As reported by America Civil Liberties Union (2022) "nearly 60,000 youth under age 18 are incarcerated in juvenile jails and prisons in the United States." Federal Bureau of Prison (2018) illustrates this situation more statistically thus: Age: 26-30 (12.2%); Age: 31-35 (16.9%); Age: 36-40 (17.9%); Age: 41-45 (16.3%); Age 46-50 (11.8%); Age: 51-55 (8.0%); Age: 56-60 (5.4%); Age: 61-65 (3.2%) and Age: 65 & above (2.7%). This statistical illustration clearly shows that the predominant ages currently in prison are between ages: 20-45 besides the regular average 60,000 teenagers within the Juvenile and some adult centers.

Matching up the above in consonance with R.K. Merton's strain theory, **societal structures can pressure individuals into committing crimes**. His Classic Strain Theory predicts that deviance is likely to happen when there is a misalignment between the "cultural goals" (and the means to attain them).

Central around social (strain) factors among which is breakaway from healthy family socialization in the process of upbringing, mental health problems become a menace and the impact is more deeply in the course of incarceration. To connect this more succinctly, one of the commonest reasons average young adults go to jail in America, aside uncultured aggression and theft, is drug related. The drug-life builds from the culture of gangling and in their ability to find the sense of belonging for themselves due to common upbringing in family disorientation. The pathway to find where to belong with the need to be relevant gravitates to drug peddling. Criminal organizations, identified as organized crime, hold this area of crime and make a lot of money by producing and selling illegal drugs. The people who work for these organizations are also lured by the cash involved in the illicit business aside gaining the chance to pleasure themselves in doing drugs. With the new-found and paying activities, not many young adults can resist the money and the promissory pleasure regardless of consequences. By the realities in the game, young adults end up in jail with high potency for socio-psychological and mental disruptions: (i) relating to separation from their newly engaging life with fellow gangs in drugdealing sub-culture (ii) relating to pre-existing lack of healthy family upbringing and relationships (iii) relating to sudden changes to their list of perceived freedom(s) and (iv) relating to their unexpressed youthful energy and monotony-routine of imprisonment, among other leading factors to mental breakdown.

This study will attempt a guided approach to the philosophies of mental illness as well as its historical analogy within the United States. It will approach the concept of criminal justice in similar manner. It will protrude the two concepts to finding the intertwines and identify areas of regression through which the earlier appears to captiously impact the core objectives of the latter, especially as relating to greater loop for recidivism in the process of corrections. The study will further identify areas of challenges in the implementation of "Rasho vs. Baldwin" programming needs, which has largely hinged on material resources, man-power and/or supply-pull of professionals needed, besides the fear embedded in the proposed asymmetric measures, which continue to shrink correctional control capacity in the process of treating mentally ill offenders within the correctional settings. The study will identify the scrutinizing efforts of IDOC management and salute the commitment of the state in budgetization and boundless expenditure at the fore of managing mental health treatment in corrections. Also, the study will recognize the judicial effort in progression towards enhancing the process of corrections through its workings. It will also attempt an appraisal of the court system for more collaborative gestures in understanding the necessity to assist correctional institution towards implementing its primary mission of positive reentry and/or restoration without building complexity for increased recidivism. The study will project a more humane campaign to de-escalation process within the correctional setting towards gaining positive compliance with SMI individuals-in-custody. It will also attempt a review of reported daily stressor-incidents that are recidivism potent, which correctional staff cope with on a routine basis in the course of duties. The book will make recommendations and equally afford the readers topical supervisory training memos towards enhancing the process of safety and security while beefing up the resource based of the agency.

Chapter Two

2.0 Federal Monitor's Report (2017 Edition) – Highlighted Defaults

The Pablo Stewart, MD's First Monitor-Report on IDOC's Implementation of "Rasho vs. Baldwin" agreement identified the following areas of compliance-defaults in the 2017 monitor-reports. It enumerated:

(i) Default in custody staff being noted to be acting as "gate keepers" when a mentally ill offender requested to be seen by the Crisis Intervention Team.

(ii) Default in medication delivery, recording, side effects monitoring, lab work, patient informed, noncompliance follow-up.

(iii) Default in the manner at which mental health professionals disclose information to patient(s).

(iv) Default in the conditions of segregation for mentally ill offenders, which remained problematic as noted throughout the monitoring period.

(v)   Default in having no formal mechanism for identifying those mentally ill offenders who were decompensating while on segregation status.

(vi)   Default in MHPs not sufficiently advocating for the mentally ill offenders in the disciplinary process.

(vii)   Default in having no timely psychiatric evaluations of mentally ill offenders who are prescribed psychotropic medications.

(viii)   Default in conducting sufficient amount of psychiatric services.

(ix)   Default in implementing the protocol to have state employee, at each facility, to supervise State clinical staff, monitor and approve vendor staff.

(x)   Default in complying with transferring Medical Records and medication with patient(s) or Individuals-in-Custody during inter-facilities transfers.

(xi)   Default in making available copies of all policies/procedures/ADs specified in Settlement Agreement – drafts to Plaintiffs and Monitor.

(xii)   Defaults in sustaining confidentiality in relation to mental health records and information.

(xiii)   Defaults in adherence to policies and training requirements.

(xiv)   Default in Behavior Treatment Program pilot.

(xv)   Default in Suicide Prevention measures.

(xvi)   Default in application of discipline in line with policies related to self-injury.

(xvii) Default in making sustainable arrangement for early delivery of Psychotropic medications; lack of consistent reviews of the supplies as well as review of related documentation.

(xviii) Default in timely availability of Treatment Plans.

(xix) Lack of reasonable time for Psychiatric Review frequency.

(xx) Lack of reasonable time for Follow-up after Specialized Treatment Settings.

(xxi) Lack of reasonable time for SMI Housing Assignment information and consultation.

(xxii) Default in application of the use of Force and verbal Abuse.

(xxiii) Default in ensuring the disciplinary system conforms with the provisions of AD 05.12.103.

(xxiv) Default relating to quality Improvement in Program implementation.

(xxv) Poor organization of medical records.

(xxvi) Default in ensuring staff improves in education and awareness relating to mental illness and commitment to the Rasho reforms.

(xxvii) "IDOC is also not meeting the requirements of the Settlement Agreement regarding the transition of offenders from specialized treatment settings " says Pablo.

This report compelled the District Court for the Central District of Illinois in Peoria Division, presided over by Judge Michael M. Mihm and Magistrate Judge Jonathan E. Hawley to issue the injunction that has largely kept the state and Illinois

Department of Corrections pressured. Assuredly pressured, in search of solution to satisfying the illimitable growth in demands for mental health care among the expanding number of individuals-in-custody across IDOC facilities within the state. Nevertheless, the monitoring reports did identify lack and inadequacy in resource-availability (both human and capital) as a major debacle to fulfilling the court's bidding.

Reviewing the entire Pablo Stewart, MD's report criminogenically however, caution must be exercised in understanding the goals of corrections. In knowing that pre-occupying Correctional department with mental health treatment burdens without thorough consideration for the goals of retribution, rehabilitation and deterrence in view of positive reentry embedded in its mission will put the larger society in limbo of safety. Because where the approach to treating mental illness preaches palliation and assuagement, correctional treatment approach pushes for adaptation and conditioning to sustain behavioral adjustment. This understanding must be taking into cognizance in the review (and rereview) of the entire implementation of the injunction to avoid the risk of drifting the focus of correctional institution from its primary mission of treating criminal minds to becoming mental health care facilities across the state.

Chapter Three

3.0 Historical Concept of Criminal Justice

Stated by Criminal Lawyer Group (2021) Penalties and the Justice System (has continued to deplete historically). At first, the purpose was simply about punishment or removal of a threat from the community, next, it was shame and restrictions as deterrence. Modern theories build it up to rehabilitation and restoration. Now, correctional focus within the Justice System in America is gradually gravitating towards mental health monitoring and management. Unfortunately, there has not been commensurate and active program deployment to care for the continuing socio-phobic and psychological effects which the victims of crime suffer. There are far less initiatives to help the innocent victim(s) survive similar depression and psychotic issues while those who victimized them enchant the attention of the court and force majeure state budgetary expenditures to enrich their course. This modernized approach to criminal justice is intertwined with the ills of capitalism in structuralism, which according to Karl Marx, may destroy itself.

In accordance with established theories, there are five (5) cardinal fundamentals of corrections (Imprisonment) as the edge-institution in criminal justice system. These fundamentals include: retribution, incapacitation, rehabilitation, deterrence, and restoration. (i) Retribution: according to codify law it is the act of punishing someone for their actions. An example of retribution is when someone gets the death penalty for committing murder. (ii) Incapacitation: It is simply the act of making an individual "incapable" of committing a crime (more crime within the society through incarceration). (iii) Rehabilitation: This is the process where an incarcerated individual is assisted towards recovery of needed values and training to enable him/her being a better person. Rehabilitation simply helps someone to get back, keep, or improve the abilities which he/she needs for daily life. (iv) Deterrence: This is an act or a process of deterring (discouraging an action) the inhibition of criminal behavior through fear of punishment. (v) Restoration: This is an act of bringing back, reinstatement or reintegration of offenders with families and/or the larger society after satisfying the process of corrections.

Going by the above fundamentals of corrections and/or incarceration; it is certain; correctional institution is not a day-care facility. Rather, it is a regimented formation, which should be treated as one. This is why the initiative to have the Department of Human Services in Illinois spearheads the mental illness treatment at the newly established in-patient center is not a misplaced priority. The initiative will help correctional authority to focus on the aspect of corrections while Human services will champion the course of addressing the mental illness with applicable treatment. This approach should help against the risk of depletion. In that refocusing correctional system on mental illness treatment and management will leave its fundamental objectives susceptible. This balancing should also serve to ensure that the basic understanding is not elusive.

In line with the tenet of justice, there was first a sentencing fiat which correctional institution is established to implement with guided policy and towards the goal of reformation. The progression into added responsibility should not at any rate drift away focus to neglecting the primary disposition of the law which sustains the fact that the SMI patients are first and foremost "offenders" who are in demand of treatment for mental illness. Going by the current shift in attention towards mental health care for incarcerated persons therefore, this fundamental understanding becomes imperative to balancing the goal of corrections with humanitarian care. The later (MH Treatment need) cannot also be treated as above the former (correctional treatment need) due to associated risks. Such risks may not be limited to: vulnerability of the correctional system, depletion of correctional objectives and goals, redefinition of Criminal Justice process, "the justification-mark" on the concept of "Justice," redefinition of reward vs deterrence, the position of the victims and the socio-economic cost of recidivism. Hence, the basic nitty-gritty of corrections and incarceration cannot be overemphasized in ensuring offenders do not manipulate the process of justice and/or complicate the system of justice.

By way of definition then, Justice means giving each person what he or she deserves. Better still, Justice is giving each person his or her due. This is regarded as Justice and fairness. As a concept, Justice can be regarded as moral uprightness; based on ethics, rationality, natural law, religion, equity and fairness. In the administration of codified law, justice is the same as fairness, taking into account the inalienable and inborn rights of all human beings and citizens. That is, the right of all people and individuals to equal protection before the law. Where those who go against the law are fairly treated in accordance with the provision of same law without sentiment in the process of implementation.

On the other hand, Criminal Justice is a system. It is the system that prescribes the fate of the criminal. It is also the system that provides recompense to the victim under the rule of law. Primarily, criminal justice seeks to deter future crimes by creating penalties for criminal conduct and rehabilitate criminals through incarceration. The three main institutions within the criminal justice system include: the law enforcement, the courts, and the corrections. Expectedly, these institutions are required to work together to prevent and punish deviant behavior. Additionally, the (fundamental) purpose of the criminal justice system is to protect the society, punish offenders and rehabilitate criminals. The system fulfills this mission by following through this process. It is a process where the offender is arrested (by law enforcement agent) and tried (by the court) for what he/she does wrong. If found guilty, the offender is punished with jail time (correctional institution) or through other punishments such as fines or community service. Nevertheless, correctional process begins at sentencing. From the time an offender is initially assessed, through case management and to supervision in the community. Hence, Correction can be best defined as the supervision of persons arrested for, convicted of, or sentenced for criminal offenses (*Terrill, 2015*).

3.1 Historical Development of Criminal Justice

Historically, the first criminal justice system was created by the British during American Revolution. The British primarily utilized hanging system to punish the convicts. The British also utilized some sub-division called districts. The head of a district was a magistrate. Compare to modern day practice, such a district head would be a judge. The Judges gathered pieces of evidence for the British government against potential criminals. Based on the evidence, a criminal may be hung, locked up or assigned to cleaning the ships.

(a) **Pre-Modern Europe Called the Dark-Age**
    In the pre-modern Europe called the Dark-age; the primary form of state-administered punishment was banishment or exile. For the most part, crime was viewed as a private matter. This view was peculiar to Ancient Greece and Rome. Even with offenses as serious as murder, justice was the prerogative of the victim's family. Predominantly, the course of justice was regarded as a private war or vendetta. This

was regarded as a way of sustaining protection against criminality.

Greece exhibited what is regarded as policing role today by deploying publicly owned slaves to guard public meetings. The magistrates also used these slaves in Ancient Greece. Specifically, in Athens, a group of 300 Scythian slaves were used to keep order, to make arrest and for crowd control. Although there was never an actual police force in the city of Rome, but the Roman Empire had a reasonably effective law enforcement system until the decline of the empire.

During that Middle Ages, crime and punishment were also dealt with through blood feuds. Blood feud was regarded as trial by ordeal. The victim and the criminal were the parties in a blood feud. Payment to the victim(s) (or their family), known as 'wergild' was a common punishment. Even in incident regarding violent crimes, criminals could restitute by paying heavy monetary fine. Criminals who could not afford to restitute through this payment-punishment system usually faced harsh penalties including corporal punishment. These penalties were not limited to: mutilation, whipping, branding, and flogging (*Hunter, 1994*).

(b) Criminal justice in Colonial America

During the colonial era in America, many parts of the criminal justice process were similar to those in England but due to lack of legal luminaries, the same process was not as effective as it was in England, based on practice. The colonial administrators did not navigate the west with their legal experts. Most of the punishments during this era were public, with the use of shame or shaming to cause deterrence. Whipping, branding, cutting of ears and placing offenders in the pillory are other forms of punishments implemented during that era. Executions were less common in Colonial America than in Europe. The main goal of these punishments however was to teach a lesson. Most deviants were mostly male. Only in cases related to witchcraft and adultery were female deviants found.

Demographically, the lower ranking members of the society were mostly the culprits. Offenders' trial in colonial America was bizarre. The typical process involved reportage of crime through the sheriff. The Sheriff forwarded documentation of crime to the magistrate who examined the evidence as presented. If commission of an offence is established, the accused would be apprehended and interrogated. The magistrate conducted this interrogation in his own house usually. No defense attorney was necessary at this trial and the proceedings moved quickly as each witness testified against the defendant.

On the overall, criminal matters were not the top priority of the colonial master in America. It was uneconomical to pursue such projects such as investing in building estates to keep custody of criminals and/or the cost of providing security-watch to sustaining it. Criminal Justice in Colonial era was molded to fit the colonialist's needs as they settled further and further west. In fact, vigilantism was said to be an inevitable by-product of the faulty and ineffective criminal justice system during colonial America, since the colonists had to find a way to cater for their own protection needs. The Sherriff had other responsibilities. This included collection of taxes. The Sherriff also ran and supervised elections. The office of the Sheriff was also used to handle other legal business in the community. Although, he followed up on complaints or information of misconduct from neighbors and other citizens, but he could only be paid through a system of fees rather than a set salary. His remuneration came mainly from the taxes he received. This discouraged the office of the Sheriff from concentrating heavily on law enforcement.

By seventeenth century, the process of common law became predominant. The common law system included a set of rules that were used to solve problems in society. It was based on the history of decisions previous judges had made instead of lawmaking codes or laws. This system made a distinction between two basic types of crimes: felonies and misdemeanors *(Eck and Takács, 2003)*. Judges, during this era performed multiple roles within the society. They were known as magistrates or justices of the peace. Yet, they were usually religious or political leaders. Judges operated within their counties as county-judges based on the county they lived in as individual judges. These Judges also adhered more with the principle of divinity. The judges believed their role was to enforce God's will. This belief system gave rise to the principle of confession and repentance from the accused rather than just punishment. The objective of this criminal justice approach was to bring order back to the society through acknowledgement of wrongdoing and sobriety. Colonial courts were much simpler and informal compare to what was practiced in England at the time. The early jails were mainly used for holding people who were awaiting trials. It was not designed as a part of punishment for the offence committed since the accused were yet to be tried. The jails were mere ordinary houses and had no distinctive control measures and/ or features. Most of the accused were lodged in normal rooms as against cell placement. There were no classifications for age or gender. Both male and female were mixed in the holding jails. This was the least of the problems facing the existence of jails in that period.

(c) **The birth of the current era in criminal justice system**

The birth of the current US criminal justice system remains a monumental hallmark in the history of the country. The re-arrangement to British colonial era Criminal Justice practices within the American states was basically orchestrated by the adoption of the Bill of Rights in 1791. The first 10 amendments to the Constitution reset basis for specific rights and freedoms of persons. It sets the rules for due process in the application of the law. This distinctly redesigned the Justice System of today.

Chapter Four

4.0 IDOC Acts of Establishment: Unified Code of Corrections

As maintained by the Legislative Reference Bureau, IDOC sustains compliant status in the Public Acts identified as: CORRECTIONS (730 ILCS 5/) or Unified Code of Corrections.

(a) **General Provisions**: This Code shall be known and may be cited as the Unified Code of Corrections (Source: P.A. 77-2097.).

(b) **Purposes**: The purposes of this Code of Corrections are to:

(i) prescribe sanctions proportionate to the seriousness of the offenses and permit the recognition of differences in rehabilitation possibilities among individual offenders;

(ii) forbid and prevent the commission of offenses;

(iii) prevent arbitrary or oppressive treatment of persons adjudicated offenders or delinquents; and

(iv) restore offenders to useful citizenship. (Source: P.A. 77-2097.)

(c) **Department of Corrections**: Defining "Department" under this classification, it means both the Department of Corrections and the Department of Juvenile Justice of the State, unless the context is specific to either the Department of Corrections or the Department of Juvenile Justice.

(d) **Consolidation of the Department:** Consolidation implies the statute of certain powers and duties of the Department of Corrections as enshrined in (730 ILCS 5/3-2-1) (from Ch. 38, par. 1003-2-1 & 2) Sec. 32-1 & 2). The following are the Powers and duties of the Department as provided by the law:

(i)   To accept persons committed to it by the courts of the State: for care, custody, treatment and rehabilitation, and

(ii) to accept federal prisoners and aliens over whom the Office of the Federal Detention Trustee is authorized to exercise the federal detention function for limited purposes and periods of time.

(iii) To develop and maintain reception and evaluation units for purposes of analyzing the custody and rehabilitation needs of persons committed to it and to assign such persons to institutions and programs under its control or transfer them to other appropriate agencies. In consultation with the Department of Alcoholism and Substance Abuse (now the Department of Human Services), the Department of Corrections shall develop a master plan for the screening and evaluation of persons committed to its custody who have alcohol or drug abuse problems, and for making appropriate treatment available to such persons; the Department shall report to the General Assembly on such plan (...). The maintenance and implementation of such plan shall be contingent upon the availability of funds.

(iv)   To create and implement (...) a pilot program to establish the effectiveness of pupillometer technology (the measurement of the pupil's reaction to light) as an alternative to a urine test for purposes of screening and evaluating persons committed to its custody who have alcohol or drug problems. The pilot program shall require the pupillometer technology to be used in at least one Department of Correctional facility. The Director may expand the pilot program to include an additional facility or facilities as he or she deems appropriate. A minimum of 4,000 tests shall be included in the pilot program. The Department must report to the General Assembly on the effectiveness of the program (...).

(v)   To develop, in consultation with the Department of State Police, a program for tracking and evaluating each inmate from commitment through release for recording his or her gang affiliations, activities, or ranks.

(vi)   To maintain and administer all State correctional institutions and facilities under its control and to establish new ones as needed. Pursuant to its power to establish new institutions and facilities, the Department may, with the written approval of the Governor, authorize the Department of Central Management

(vii)   Services to enter into an agreement of the type described in subsection (d) of Section 405-300 of the Department of Central Management Services Law (20 ILCS 405/405-300). The Department shall designate those institutions which shall constitute the State Penitentiary System. The Department of Juvenile Justice shall maintain and administer all State youth centers pursuant to subsection (d) of Section 3-2.5-20.

(viii)   Pursuant to its power to establish new institutions and facilities, the Department may authorize the Department of Central Management Services to accept bids from counties and municipalities for the construction, remodeling or conversion of a structure to be leased to the Department of Corrections for the purposes of its serving as a correctional institution or facility. Such construction, remodeling or conversion may be financed with revenue bonds issued pursuant to the Industrial Building Revenue Bond Act by the municipality or county. The lease specified in a bid shall be for a term of not less than the time needed to retire any revenue bonds used to finance the project, but not to exceed 40 years. The lease may grant to the State the option to purchase the structure outright.

(ix)   Upon receipt of the bids, the Department may certify one or more of the bids and shall submit any such bids to the General Assembly for approval. Upon approval of a bid by a constitutional majority of both houses of the General Assembly, pursuant to joint resolution, the Department of Central Management Services may enter into an agreement with the county or municipality pursuant to such bid.

(x)   To build and maintain regional juvenile detention centers and to charge a per diem to the counties as established by the Department to defray the costs of housing each minor in a center. In this subsection, "juvenile detention center" means a facility to house minors during pendency of trial who have been transferred from proceedings under the Juvenile Court Act of 1987 to prosecutions under the criminal laws of this State in accordance with Section 5-805 of the Juvenile Court Act of 1987, whether the transfer was by operation of law or permissive under that Section. The Department shall designate the counties to be served by each regional juvenile detention center.

(xi)   To develop and maintain programs of control, rehabilitation and employment of committed persons within its institutions.

(xii)   To provide a pre-release job preparation program for inmates at Illinois adult correctional centers.

(xiii) To provide educational and visitation opportunities to committed persons within its institutions through temporary access to content-controlled tablets that may be provided as a privilege to committed persons to induce or reward compliance.

(xiv)   To establish a system of supervision and guidance of committed persons in the community.

(xv)   To establish in cooperation with the Department of Transportation to supply a sufficient number of prisoners for use by the Department of Transportation to clean up the trash and garbage along State, county, township, or municipal highways as designated by the Department of Transportation. The Department of Corrections, at the request of the Department of Transportation, shall furnish such prisoners at least annually for a period to be agreed upon between the Director of Corrections and the Secretary of Transportation. The prisoners used on this program shall be selected by the Director of Corrections on whatever basis he deems proper in consideration of their term, behavior and earned eligibility to participate in such program - where they will be outside of the prison facility but still in the custody of the Department of Corrections. Prisoners convicted of firstdegree murder, or a Class X felony, or armed violence, or aggravated kidnapping, or criminal sexual assault, aggravated criminal sexual abuse or a subsequent conviction for criminal sexual abuse, or forcible detention, or arson, or a prisoner adjudged a Habitual Criminal shall not be eligible for selection to participate in such program. The prisoners shall remain as prisoners in the custody of the Department of Corrections and such Department shall furnish whatever security is necessary. The Department of Transportation shall furnish trucks and equipment for the highway cleanup program and personnel to supervise and direct the program. Neither the Department of Corrections nor the Department of Transportation shall replace any regular employee with a prisoner.

(xvi) To maintain records of persons committed to it and to establish programs of research, statistics and planning.

(xvii) To investigate the grievances of any person committed to the Department and to inquire into any alleged misconduct by employees or committed persons; and for these purposes it may issue subpoenas and compel the attendance of witnesses and the production of writings and papers, and may examine under oath any witnesses who may appear before it; to also investigate alleged violations of a parolee's or releasee's conditions of parole or release; and for this purpose it may issue subpoenas and compel the attendance of witnesses and the production of documents only if there is reason to believe that such procedures would provide evidence that such violations have occurred. If any person fails to obey a subpoena issued under this subsection, the Director may apply to any circuit court to secure compliance with the subpoena. The failure to comply with the order of the court issued in response thereto shall be punishable as contempt of court.

(xviii) To appoint and remove the chief administrative officers and administer programs of training and development of personnel of the Department. Personnel assigned by the Department to be responsible for the custody and control of committed persons or to investigate the alleged misconduct of committed persons or employees or alleged violations of a parolee's or releasee's conditions of parole shall be conservators of the peace for those purposes, and shall have the full power of peace officers outside of the facilities of the Department in the protection, arrest, retaking and reconfining of committed persons or where the exercise of such power is necessary to the investigation of such misconduct or violations. This subsection shall not apply to persons committed to the Department of Juvenile Justice under the Juvenile Court Act of 1987 on aftercare release.

(xix) To cooperate with other departments and agencies and with local communities for the development of standards and programs for better correctional services in this State.

(xx) To administer all moneys and properties of the Department.

(xxi) To report annually to the Governor on the committed persons, institutions and programs of the Department.

(xxii) To make all rules and regulations and exercise all powers and duties vested by law in the Department.

(xxiii) To establish rules and regulations for administering a system of sentence credits, established in accordance with Section 3-6-3, subject to review by the Prisoner Review Board.

(xxiv) To administer the distribution of funds from the State Treasury to reimburse counties where State penal institutions are located for the payment of assistant state's attorneys' salaries under Section 42001 of the Counties Code.

(xxv) To exchange information with the Department of Human Services and the Department of Healthcare and Family Services for the purpose of verifying living arrangements and for other purposes directly connected with the administration of this Code and the Illinois Public Aid Code.

(xxvi) To establish a diversion program. The program shall provide a structured environment for selected technical parole or mandatory supervised release violators and committed persons who have violated the rules governing their conduct while in work release. This program shall not apply to those persons who have committed a new offense while serving on parole or mandatory supervised release or while committed to work release.

Elements of the program shall include, but shall not be limited to, the following:

- The staff of a diversion facility shall provide supervision in accordance with required objectives set by the facility.
- Participants shall be required to maintain employment
- Each participant shall pay for room and board at the facility on a sliding-scale basis according to the participant's income.

- Each participant shall: provide restitution to victims in accordance with any court order; provide financial support to his dependents; and make appropriate payments toward any other court-ordered obligations; shall complete community service in addition to employment; take part in such counseling, educational and other programs as the Department may deem appropriate; submit to drug and alcohol screening; promulgate rules governing the administration of the program

(xxvii) To enter into intergovernmental cooperation agreements under which persons in the custody of the Department may participate in a county impact incarceration program established under Section 3-6038 or 3-15003.5 of the Counties Code.

(xxviii) To systematically and routinely identify with respect to each street-gang active within the correctional system: (1) each active gang; (2) every existing inter-gang affiliation or alliance; and (3) the current leaders in each gang. The Department shall promptly segregate leaders from inmates who belong to their gangs and allied gangs. "Segregate" means no physical contact and, to the extent possible under the conditions and space available at the correctional facility, prohibition of visual and sound communication. For the purposes of this paragraph, "leaders" means persons who: (i) are members of a criminal street-gang; (ii) with respect to other individuals within the street-gang, occupy a position of organizer, supervisor, or other position of management or leadership; and (iii) are actively and personally engaged in directing, ordering, authorizing, or requesting commission of criminal acts by others which are punishable as a felony, in furtherance of street-gang related activity both within and outside of the Department of Corrections. "Streetgang", "gang", and "street-gang related" have the meanings ascribed to them in Section 10 of the Illinois Street-gang Terrorism Omnibus Prevention Act.

(xxix) To operate a super-maximum security institution, in order to manage and supervise inmates who are disruptive or dangerous and provide for the safety and security of the staff and the other inmates.

(xxx) To monitor any unprivileged conversation or any unprivileged communication, whether in person or by mail, telephone, or other means, between an inmate who, before commitment to the Department, was a member of an organized gang and any other person without the need to show cause or satisfy any other requirement of law before beginning the monitoring, except as constitutionally required. The monitoring may be by video, voice, or other method of recording or by any other means. As used in this subdivision), "organized gang" has the meaning ascribed to it in Section 10 of the Illinois Street gang Terrorism Omnibus Prevention Act.

(xxxi) As used in this section, "unprivileged conversation" or "unprivileged communication" means a conversation or communication that is not protected by any privilege recognized by law or by decision, rule, or order of the Illinois Supreme Court.

(xxxii) To establish a Women's and Children's Pre-release Community Supervision Program for the purpose of providing housing and services to eligible female inmates, as determined by the Department, and their newborn and young children.

(xxxiii) To issue an order, whenever a person committed to the Department absconds or absents himself or herself, without authority to do so, from any facility or program to which he or she is assigned. The order shall be certified by the Director, the Supervisor of the Apprehension Unit, or any person duly designated by the Director, with the seal of the Department affixed. The order shall be directed to all sheriffs, coroners, and police officers, or to any particular person named in the order. Any order issued pursuant to this shall be sufficient warrant for the officer or person named in the order to arrest and deliver the committed person to the proper correctional officials and shall be executed the same as criminal process.

(xxxiv) To do all other acts necessary to carry out the provisions of this (Act):

- The Department of Corrections shall (…) consider building and operating a correctional facility within 100 miles of a county of over 2,000,000 inhabitants, especially a facility designed to house juvenile participants in the impact incarceration program.
- When the Department lets bids for contracts for medical services to be provided to persons committed to Department facilities by a health maintenance organization, medical service corporation, or other health care provider, the bid may only be let to a health care provider that has obtained an irrevocable letter of credit or performance bond issued by a company whose bonds have an investment grade or higher rating by a bond rating organization.
- When the Department lets bids for contracts for food or commissary services to be provided to Department facilities, the bid may only be let to a food or commissary

services provider that has obtained an irrevocable letter of credit or performance bond issued by a company whose bonds have an investment grade or higher rating by a bond rating organization.

- On and after the date 6 months after August 16, 2013 (the effective date of Public Act 98-488), as provided in the Executive Order 1 (2012)

- Implementation Act, all of the powers, duties, rights, and responsibilities related to State healthcare purchasing under this Code that were transferred from the Department of Corrections to the Department of Healthcare and Family Services by Executive Order 3 (2005) are transferred back to the Department of Corrections; however, powers, duties, rights, and responsibilities related to State healthcare purchasing under this Code that were exercised by the Department of Corrections before the effective date of Executive Order 3 (2005) but that pertain to individuals resident in facilities operated by the Department of Juvenile Justice are transferred to the Department of Juvenile Justice. (Source: P.A. 101-235, eff. 1-1-20; 102-350, eff. 8-13-21.)

4.1 Report of violence in Department of Corrections' institutions & facilities/Public safety reports (Sec. 3-2-12 of (730 ILCS 5/3-2-12)

The public safety reports within the Department shall be as follow:

(a) The Department of Corrections shall collect and report: data on a rate per 100 of committed persons regarding violence within Department institutions and facilities as defined under the terms, if applicable, in 20 Ill. Adm. Code 504 as follows:

- committed person on committed person assaults;
- committed person on correctional staff assaults; - dangerous contraband, including weapons, explosives, dangerous chemicals, or other dangerous weapons;
- committed person on committed person fights;
- multi-committed person on single committed person fights;
- committed person use of a weapon on correctional staff;
- committed person use of a weapon on committed person;
- sexual assault committed by a committed person against another committed person, correctional staff, or visitor;

- sexual assault committed by correctional staff against another correctional staff, committed person, or visitor;
- correctional staff use of physical force;
- forced cell extraction;
- use of oleoresin capsicum (pepper spray), - use of chlorobenzalmalononitrile (CS gas), or other control agents or implements;
- committed person suicide and attempted suicide; - requests and placements in protective custody; and
- committed persons in segregation, secured housing, and restrictive housing; and

(b) The Department of Corrections shall collect and report:

- data on a rate per 100 of committed persons regarding public safety as follows: (i) committed persons released directly from segregation secured housing and restrictive housing to the community; (ii) the types of housing facilities, whether private residences, transitional housing, homeless shelters, or other, to which committed persons are released from Department correctional institutions and facilities; (iii) committed persons in custody who have completed evidence-based programs, including: educational; vocational; chemical dependency; sex offender treatment; or cognitive behavioral; (iv) committed persons who are being held in custody past their mandatory statutory release date and the reasons for their continued confinement; (v) parole and mandatory supervised release revocation rate by county and reasons for revocation; and (vi) committed persons on parole or mandatory supervised release who have completed evidence-based programs, including: educational; vocational; chemical dependency; sex offender treatment; or cognitive behavioral; and

- data on the average daily population and vacancy rate of each Adult Transition Center and work camp.

(c) All data provided under subsections (a) and (b) above shall be included in the Department of Corrections quarterly report to the General Assembly under Section 3-5-3.1 of this Code and shall include an aggregate chart at the agency level and individual reports by each correctional institution or facility of the Department of Corrections.

(d) The Director of Corrections shall ensure that the agency level data is reviewed by the Director's executive team on a quarterly basis. The correctional institution or facility's executive team and each chief administrative officer of the correctional institution or facility shall examine statewide and local data at least quarterly. During these reviews, each chief administrative officer shall:

(1) identify trends;

(2) develop action items to mitigate the root causes of violence; and

(3) establish committees at each correctional institution or facility which shall review the violence data on a quarterly basis and develop action plans to reduce violence. These plans shall include a wide range of strategies to incentivize good conduct.
(Source: P.A. 100-907, eff. 1-1-19; 101-81, eff. 7-12-19.)

A review of the above provisions in the acts indicates that the use of restrictive housing, segregation time, chemical agent and/or use of force are correctional tools bestowed by the acts and guided by established policies to sustain controls within institutional facilities and for purposes of safety and security of persons and state property. This understanding must be shared to guide perception and interpretation of statutory responsibility of the department. Especially more, when individuals, group of individuals or opinionists outside the department demonstrate eagerness in making contributions relating to correctional measures of control for compliance.

For instance, the "news story" below was sourced from an online publication, reporting a particular incident which was purportedly cited as corroborative incident report during a court session against the department of correction.

"On Dec. 21, 2015, Molly, then 23 years old, climbed the fence of Logan Correctional Center in Lincoln, Illinois, where she had been incarcerated since 2013.

(To protect Molly's identity, only her first name is being used – According to the online source of this news story.) "I'm not trying to escape, I just wanted to cut myself," she told the officers, according to a disciplinary report. She used the razor wire from the fence to cut her arm.

She was pepper sprayed and charged with disobeying a direct order to come down. Her punishment was one month of restricted recreation" (Weill-Greenberg, 2018).

To sustain this tempo of empathy against correctional practices, another opinionist stated as follow: "if you look at the misconduct as a symptom of an illness, the first reaction should be, 'How do we up the amount of treatment that somebody is getting?' Because clearly they're not getting either enough or the right kind of treatment," Mills said, (Mills in Christine, 2018) and stated furthered, 'it is like withholding aspirin from a person who has a fever until their temperature goes away."

Showing understanding with these humanitarian dispositions however does not change the course of the law and/or the tenets of justice. For instance, reanalyzing some of the firsthand information acquired from some of the committed persons in the course of their individualized moments may help understanding to enhance comprehension of totality of circumstance. The example cited below in reaction to Molly's scenario above may assist (some outsider-analysts) to understand reasons behind certain action taken by Correctional employees when his/her committed person is acting up in some kind of way. It is also important to understand that these typical correctional employees are the primary responders who see it all, due to the condition of their job-functions, being around the committed persons every hour of the day.

To attempt a narrative of one of such field experiences; an individual-in-custody designated as SMI called his designated correctional watch-officer after landing in outside hospital as a result of serious self-harming behavior. The SMI "Patient" stated: *"Hey guy, don't take this personal and feel like I am stressing you out. I have got to do what I have got to do to establish I am psychotic. I have got court session coming up in about a month. I don't want any more sanctions. I have got to act up many times before my hearing. Please just document."* Access to this nature of statement as a result of work-related closeness does inform the likelihood for a typical correctional employee to seeing such committed person differently than other persons out there. Realistically speaking, the way other individuals (external monitors) may feel more sympathetic about same committed person especially during a situation of psychotic episode may be different from the way that correctional staff who was directly spoken to may perceive the same SMI Patient. As a criminal justice institution therefore the department of corrections has an obligation to perform its mandates by taking into cognizance the criminogenic attributes of the individuals-in-custody who are serving terms under its managerial authority. It is also in the performance of these responsibilities as the justice agent that the society can be safeguarded.

Another concern that must also be taken into cognizance is the perception of the victim of crime. According to *Latarski* (2020) who posted as a victim of crime, in his exacerbating remarks, he stated: "No violent criminal should be allowed multiple appeals, or take in excess of 2-5 years coming to trial. Technical aspects eliminating crucial evidence should not be allowed. Approximately 77% to 80% incarcerated persons ended up back in jail committing similar or worse crimes, murder included. Criminals are provided gyms to bulk up and make them stronger to commit their crimes. Law libraries are provided to allow jail-house lawyers to submit appeal after appeal, and of course there are the niceties to provide comfort & entertainment; government converting prisons to vacation (lodge-inn) and complaining they are coming back? All of which puts a financial burden on taxpayers and the system. Progressives call for gun control. (…) Lawlessness and violent crimes are becoming the norm due to weak justice system. We are so civilized that we are committing national suicide. Those administering the system are guilty of assaulting the victims a second time."

Chapter Five

5.0 Established Policies & Procedures Instituted to Regulate Correctional Staff and Operational Activities in IDOC towards Effective Mental Health Management

The following policies and procedures are established to guide conduct and practice in IDOC. These are the presets or lay down guidance called policies which correctional staffs are expected to utilize as the mirror of conduct to guide their action(s) while providing correctional services and administering the affairs of the committed persons in IDOC. The list includes but not limited to:

(A) Administrative Directives:

(i) AD 404103: Use of Restraints for Mental Health Purposes

(ii) AD 501104 Use, Security and storage of Cameras, Digital Media and Related Equipment

(iii) AD 501113: Searches of Offenders

(iv)   AD 501126: Security Restraints

(v)   AD 404102: Suicide Prevention and Emergency Services

(vi)   AD 404125: Mental Health Continuous Quality Improvement Program

(vii)   AD 501127: Use and Control of Batons

(viii)   AD 501173: Calculated Use of Force Cell Extractions

(ix)   AD 501301: Lockdowns

(x)   AD 503105: Identifying and monitoring escape Level Designations 2021

(xi)   AD 503106 Control of Offender Movement

(xii)   AD 510110: Use and Control of Individual in Custody Storage Boxes and Commissary Items

(xiii)   AD 512101: Administrative Detention Placement

(xiv)   AD 512103: Administration of Discipline for Individual-in-Custody Designated as Seriously Mentally Ill

(xv)   AD 515100: Restrictive Housing

(xvi)   AD 107620: Calculation of Demotion and Restoration of Grades

(xvii)   AD 107805: Identification of Individual-in-Custody

(xviii)   AD 112105: Reporting of Unusual Incidents

(xix)   AD 112115 Institutional Investigations of Unusual Incidents

(xx)   AD 117103: Offender Assignments and Performance Evaluations

(xxi)   AD 301106: Housing and Maintenance

(xxii) AD 401105: Facility Orientation 2021

(xxiii) AD 401111: ADA Accommodations 2021

(xxiv) AD 401118: Individual in Custody Restriction for Disciplinary Violations

(B)   Departmental Rules:

DR 504: Discipline and Grievances Below provides details in DR 504 Offence Numbers & Definitions:

(i)   **Offence #100: Violent Assault of any Person**…causing a person, substance or object to come into contact with another in a deadly manner or in a manner that result in serious bodily injury.

(ii)   **Offence #101: Arson** … Settling fire in any location whether public or private, including, but not limited to any part of the facility, its grounds, or state vehicles.

(iii)   **Offence #102a: Assault with Injury** … causing a person, substance or object to come into contact with, and resulting in injury to, a staff member, contractual employee, official visitor, visitor or volunteer.

(iv)   **Offence #102b: Assault** … causing a person, substance or object to come into contact with a staff member, contractual employee, official visitor, visitor or volunteer in an offensive or provocative manner; or fighting with a weapon.

(v) **Offence #102c: Assault to an Offender** ...causing a person, substance or an object to come into contact with any offender in an offensive, provocative or injurious manner, or fighting with a weapon.

(vi) **Offence #103: Bribery & Extortion** ... demanding or receiving anything of value in exchange for protection, to avoid bodily injury, or through duress or pressure. Giving or receiving money or anything of value to violate state or federal law or to commit any act prohibited under this part.

(vii) **Offence #104: Dangerous Contraband** ... possessing, manufacturing, introducing, selling, supplying to others or using without authorization any explosive, acid, caustic material for incendiary devices, ammunition, dangerous chemical, escape material, knife, sharpened instrument, gun, firearm, razor, glass, bludgeon. Brass, knuckles, cutting tools, tools which may be used to defeat security measures such as hacksaw blades, keys and lock picks, any other dangerous or deadly weapon or substance of like character or any object or instrument that is in made to appear to be or could be used as a deadly or dangerous weapon or substance.

(viii) **Offence #105: Dangerous Disturbances** ...causing, directing or participating in any action or group activity that may threaten the control or security of a facility or seriously disrupt or endanger the operations of a facility, persons or property, including the taking or holding of hostages by force or threat of force and engaging in prohibited group activities such as work stoppages or hunger strikes.

(ix)   **Offence #106: Escape** ... leaving or failing to return to lawful custody without authorization, including the failure to return from furlough, leaves or authorized absence within two hours after the designated time.

(x)   **Offence #107: Sexual Misconduct** ... engaging in sexual intercourse, sexual conduct or gesturing, fondling or touching done to sexually arouse, intimidate or harass either or both persons, or engaging in any of these activities with an animal. However, private masturbation in the offenders' living area, excluding a deliberate display of the act or to affront others, shall not be considered sexual misconduct.

(xi)   **Offence #108: sexual Assault** ... causing unwilling contact between the sex organ of one person and the sex organ, mouth or anus of another person or any intrusion of any part of the body of one person or object into the sex organ or anus of another person by use of force or threat or force, including pressure, threats or any other actions or communications by one or more persons to force another person to engage in a partial or complete sexual act.

(xii)   **Offence #109: Electronic Contraband** … Possessing, selling, receiving, supplying to others, or using without authorization any electronic device, video recording device, computer or cellular communications equipment, including but not limited to, cellular telephones, cellular telephone batteries, pagers, computers and computer peripheral equipment.

(xiii)   **Offence #110: Impending Or Interfering with an investigation** … obstructing, impeding or refusing to provide information relevant to an investigation in an attempt to undermine or alter the course of the investigation.

(xiv)   **Offence #111: Security Threat Group Or Unauthorized Organizational Leadership Activity** … Knowingly accepting or assuming any leadership position or a position of authority over other offenders in any security threat group or unauthorized organization, or pressuring, recruiting, organizing authority or directing others to engage in security threat group or unauthorized organizational activities, meetings or criminal acts on behalf of an organization not approved pursuant to 20III. Adm. Code 445 or 450.

(xv)   **Offence #201: Concealment of Identity** ...wearing a disguise or a mask, impersonating another or otherwise concealing one's identity.

(xvi)   **Offence #202: Damage Or Misuse of Property** ... destroying, damaging, removing, altering, tampering with, or otherwise misusing property belonging to the state, another person or entity, including the obstruction of locks or security devices, destroying or tempering with bar codes or identification cards, or the use of another person's identification card.

(xvii)   **Offence #203: Drugs and Drug Paraphernalia** ... possessing, manufacturing, introducing, selling supplying to others, or receiving alcohol, any intoxicant, inhalant, narcotic, syringe, needle, unauthorized controlled medication, controlled substance, unidentified medication or marijuana or being under the influence of any of the above substances, or refusing to be tested for drug or alcohol to, including failure to provide a specimen within two hours after the request or destroying or tampering with drug or alcohol tests or testing equipment.

(xviii) **Offence #204: Forgery** ... forging, counterfeiting or reproducing without authorization any document, article of identification, money, security or official paper

(xix) **Offence #205: Security Threat Group Or Unauthorized Organizational Activity** ...engaging in security threat group or unauthorized organizational activities, meeting or criminal acts, displaying, wearing, possessing or using security threat group or unauthorized organizational insignia or materials; or giving security threat group or unauthorized signs

(xx) **Offence #206: Intimidation Or Threats** ... expressing by words, actions or other behavior an intent to cause harm t that person or to another will result, or any unauthorized contact or attempt to contact staff outside of official Department business.

(xxi) **Offence #208: Dangerous Communications** ... engaging in verbal or written communication that is likely to encourage violence against persons or that's likely to disrupt or endanger the safety and security of the facility, including but not limited to, escape plans and manufacture of weapons.

(xxii) **Offence #209: Dangerous Written Material** ...possessing or causing to be brought into the facility written material that presents a serious threat to the safety and security of persons or the facility, including, but not limited to, written material relating to methods of escape and the manufacturing of weapons.

(xxiii) **Offence #210: Impairment of Surveillance** ...using curtains, coverings or any other matter or object in an unauthorized manner that obstructs or otherwise impairs the line or vision into an offender's cell or room that obstructs or otherwise impairs any viewing panel or surveillance equipment, both audio and visual, within the facility.

(xxiv) **Offence #211: Possession Or Solicitation of Unauthorized Personal Information** ...possession or soliciting unauthorized personal information regarding another offender, release, employee, former employee or volunteer, including, but not limited to, personnel files, master files, medical or mental health records, photographs, social security numbers, home addresses, financial information or telephone numbers, except as authorized by a court order or as approved in writing by the Chief Administrative Officer

(xxv) **Offence #212: Frivolous Lawsuit** ... a pleading motion or other pager filed by the offender for which the court, in accordance with 730 IL CS 5/3-6-3, has found to be frivolous.

(xxvi) **Offence #213: Failure to Reveal Assets** ... failing to fully cooperate in revealing financial assets on the form provided including tangible and intangible property and real and personal property, providing false or inaccurate information regarding financial assets or dependents on the forms provided, or refusing to cooperate in revealing financial assets on the form provided

(xxvii) **Offence #214: Fighting** ... fighting with another person in a manner that is not likely to cause serious bodily injury to one or the other and that does not involve the use of a weapon.

(xxviii) **Offence #215: Disobeying a Direct Order Essential to Safety and Security** ... Willfully refusing, or rejecting to comply with, an order when continued refusal results in a use of force to maintain the safety and security of a facility. This shall include, but not limited to, refusing to submit to a search, refusing to submit to the application of mechanical restraints, refusing a designated housing assignment or refusing to leave an area.

(xxix)　**Offence #302: Gambling**… operating or playing a game of chance or skill for anything of value, making a bet upon the outcome of any event, or possessing any gambling device. This shall include participating in any lottery.

(xxx)　**Offence #303: Giving False Information to an Employee**… lying or knowingly providing false information to an employee, either orally or in writing.

(xxxi)　**Offence #304: Insolence** … Talking, touching, gesticulating or other behavior that harasses, annoys or shows disrespect.

(xxxii)　**Offence #305: Theft** …Taking property belonging to another person or entry or the facility without the owner's authorization.

(xxxiii)　**Offence #306: Transfer of Funds** … causing money to be transferred from one trust fund to another or through an outside source to the account of another offender or entering into contracts or credit agreements without written approval from the Chief Administrative Officer.

(xxxiv)　**Offence #307: Unauthorized Movement** … being anywhere without authorization or being absent from where required to be or returning late or not traveling directly to or from any authorized destination without prior staff approval.

(xxxv) **Offence #308: Contraband Or Unauthorized Property** ... possessing, giving, loaning, receiving or using property that an offender has no authorization to have or receive and that was not issued to the individual through regular procedures, including the unauthorized possession of food or clothing or the possession of property in excess of that authorized by the facility or property that has been altered from its original state. This offence includes prescribed medication misuse, such as, but not limited to, prescribed medication that is expired, loose or altered from its original state.

(xxxvi) **Offence #309: Postings and Business ventures** ... writing, signing or circulating a petition without authorization, unauthorized distributing or posting of any printed or written materials, including surveys engaging in an unauthorized business venture or representing oneself as a corporation or official of a corporation without authorization.

(xxxvii) **Offence #310: Abuse of Privileges** ... violating rule regarding visits, mail, the library, yard, commissary, telephone, authorized electronic, communication or recreational activities. This includes unauthorized telephone usage, threeparty calls, call forwarding, corresponding or communicating, by any means, with a victim, a victim's family member or any other person after the offender has received notice that such person has informed the Department that he or she does not wish to receive correspondence from the offender. However, if the conduct also constitutes a violation of federal or state law, a committed person may also be charged under #501.

(xxxviii) **Offence #311: Failure to Submit to Medical or forensic Tests** … willfully refusing to, or cooperate with testing, examination or the provision of samples requiring by court order. State law or current standards of public health and safety, including the refusal to submit to annual tuberculosis screening and mandatory HIV or DNA testing.

(xxxix) **Offence #312: Possession of Money** … possessing or causing to be brought into the facility any coin, currency or other negotiable instrument without authorization or for residents of transition centers, failure to promptly submit an income to center staff, including wages, tips, gifts or any check for social security, disability, veteran's benefits grants, scholarships or loans.

(xl) **Offence #313: Disobeying a Direct Order** … willfully refusing or neglecting to comply with an order, including the refusal to participate in educational testing, to accept a work, educational or housing assignment or to work area or other place in the facility or its grounds.

(xli)   **Offence #402: Health, Smoking or Safety Violations** …smoking, tattooing or body piercing, including but not limited to piercing of the ear, nose or lip, or disregarding basic hygiene of any person, cell, living or work area or other place in the facility or its grounds.

(xlii)   **Offence #404: Violation of Rules** …willfully disobeying any rule of the facility. If the specific offence is stated elsewhere in this Part, a committed person may not be charged with this offence. The rule violated must be specified in the disciplinary report.

(xliii)   **Offence #405: Failure to Report** …failure to report for a work, educational or program assignment or for transport.

(xliv)   **Offence #406: Trading Or Trafficking** …trading or trafficking with any person.

(xlv)   **Offence #501: Violating State Or Federal Laws** …committing any act that would constitute a violation of state or federal law. If the specific offence is stated elsewhere in this Part, an offender may not be charged with this offence except as otherwise provided in this section. The state or federal offence must be specified in the disciplinary report.

(xlvi) **Offence #601: Aiding and Abetting, Attempt, Solicitation Or Conspiracy** ...aiding and abetting any person in the commission of any of these offenses, attempting to commit any of these offenses, making plans to commit any of these offences, soliciting another to commit any of these offences, or conspiring to commit any of these offenses shall be considered the same as the commission of the offence itself and shall carry the penalty prescribed for the underlying offence. The underlying offense must be specified in the disciplinary report.

Table 5.1: Maximum Penalties for Offenders per Departmental Direction

The below disciplinary penalties are a reduction from the maximum penalties allowed under Departmental Rule 504. October 1, 2020 Revised Version.

Offense	Maximum Penalties for Offenders per Dept. Direction			
	Loss or Restriction of Privileges	B or C Grade	Sentence Credit Revocation	Segregation
100. Violent Assault of any Person	1 year	90 days	1 year	1 year
101. Arson	1 year	90 days	1 year	6 months
102a. Assault with Injury	1 year	90 days	1 year	1 year

Offense	Maximum Penalties for Offenders per Dept. Direction			
	Loss or Restriction of Privileges	B or C Grade	Sentence Credit Revocation	Segregation
102b. Assault	1 year	90 days	6 months	3 months
102c. Assault of an Offender	6 months	90 days	6 months	3 months
103. Bribery & Extortion	1 year	0 days	1 year	29 days
104. Dangerous Contraband	1 year	90 days	1 year	1 year
105. Dangerous Disturbance	1 year	90 days	1 year	6 months
106. Escape or	1 year	1 year	1 year	1 year

Offense	Maximum Penalties for Offenders per Dept. Direction			
	Loss or Restriction of Privileges	B or C Grade	Sentence Credit Revocation	Segregation
Runaway				
107. Sexual Misconduct	6 months	90 days	6 months	6 months
108. Sexual Assault	1 year	90 days	1 year	1 year
109. Electronic Contraband	1 year	90 days	1 year	3 months
110. Impeding or Interfering with an Investigation	3 months	0 days	3 months	29 days
111. Security Threat	1 year	90 days	1 year	1 year

Offense	Maximum Penalties for Offenders per Dept. Direction			
	Loss or Restriction of Privileges	B or C Grade	Sentence Credit Revocation	Segregation
Group or Unauthorized Organizational Leadership Activity				
201. Concealment of Identity	6 months	0 days	0 days	29 days
202. Damage or Misuse of Property	6 months	0 days	0 days	0 days
203. Drugs and Drug	6 months /	0 days / 1 month	6 months	6 months /

Offense		Maximum Penalties for Offenders per Dept. Direction			
		Loss or Restriction of Privileges	B or C Grade	Sentence Credit Revocation	Segregation
	Paraphernalia	1 month for intoxicants	for intoxicants		29 days for intoxicants
204.	Forgery	3 months	0 days	0 days	0 days
205.	Security Threat Group or Unauthorized Organizational Activity	6 months	0 days	0 days	29 days
206.	Intimidation or Threats	6 months	0 days	0 days	29 days

Offense		Maximum Penalties for Offenders per Dept. Direction			
		Loss or Restriction of Privileges	B or C Grade	Sentence Credit Revocation	Segregation
208.	Dangerous Communications	6 months	0 days	0 days	29 days
209.	Dangerous Written Material	6 months	0 days	0 days	29 days
210.	Impairment of Surveillance	6 months	0 days	0 days	29 days
211.	Possession or Solicitation of Unauthorized Personal	6 months	0 days	0 days	29 days

	Maximum Penalties for Offenders per Dept. Direction			
Offense	Loss or Restriction of Privileges	B or C Grade	Sentence Credit Revocation	Segregation
Information				
212. Frivolous Lawsuit	0 days	0 days	6 months	0 days
213. Failure to Reveal Assets	0 days	0 days	0 days	0 days
214. Fighting	6 months	6 months	0 days	29 days
215. Disobeying a Direct Order Essential to Safety and Security	6 months	6 months	0 days	29 days

	Maximum Penalties for Offenders per Dept. Direction			
Offense	Loss or Restriction of Privileges	B or C Grade	Sentence Credit Revocation	Segregation
302. Gambling	3 months	3 months	0 days	0 days
303. Giving False Information to an Employee	3 months	3 months	0 days	0 days
304. Insolence	3 months	3 months	0 days	0 days
305. Theft	6 months	6 months	0 days	0 days
306. Transfer of Funds	3 months	3 months	0 days	0 days

Offense	Maximum Penalties for Offenders per Dept. Direction			
	Loss or Restriction of Privileges	B or C Grade	Sentence Credit Revocation	Segregation
307. Unauthorized Movement	3 months	3 months	0 days	0 days
308. Contraband or Unauthorized Property	6 months	6 months	0 days	0 days
309. Petitions, Postings, and Business Ventures	3 months	3 months	0 days	0 days
310. Abuse of Privileges	3 months	3 months	0 days	0 days

Offense	Maximum Penalties for Offenders per Dept. Direction			
	Loss or Restriction of Privileges	B or C Grade	Sentence Credit Revocation	Segregation
311. Failure to Submit to Medical or Forensic Tests	3 months	3 months	0 days	0 days
312. Possession of Money	3 months	3 months	0 days	0 days
313. Disobeying a Direct Order	6 months	6 months	0 days	0 days
402. Health, Smoking, or Safety	3 months	3 months	0 days	0 days

| Offense | Maximum Penalties for Offenders per Dept. Direction | | | |
	Loss or Restriction of Privileges	B or C Grade	Sentence Credit Revocation	Segregation
Violations				
404. Violation of Rules	1 month	1 month	0 days	0 days
405. Failure to Report	1 month	1 month	0 days	0 days
406. Trading or Trafficking	2 months	2 months	0 days	0 days
501. Violating State or Federal Laws	1 year	90 days	1 year	1 year
601. Aiding and Abetting, Attempt,	Same as underlying	Same as underly	Same as underlying offense	½ as underlying offense
Offense	Maximum Penalties for Offenders per Dept. Direction			
	Loss or Restriction of Privileges	B or C Grade	Sentence Credit Revocation	Segregation
Solicitation, or Conspiracy	offense	ing offense		

Source: IDOC Policy Documentations https://
www.law.umich.edu/special/policyclearinghouse/
Do cuments/Illinois%20-%20Offenses%20
and%20Maximum%20Penalties.pdf

(C)   Institutional Directives (Specific for IDOC Mental Health Treatment Centers)

Establishment of Emergency Response Team (ERT): Responsibilities, Guidelines and Procedure:

Job Description: ERT Members to perform their duties under the general supervision of the Corrections Treatment Senior Security Supervisor. Tactical Commander will be direct supervisor. **Administrative Expectations of ERT**: The list includes, but not limited to:

(i)   ERT shall comply with Administrative Directive/ Institutional Directive 03.02.108 Standards of Conduct.

(ii)   ERT shall perform all assigned duties in an ethical and professional manner.

(iii) ERT shall comply with Administrative Directive and/or Institutional Directive(s), such as: (a) 05.01.101 Use and control of Tools and, (b) 05.01.103 Key and Lock Control measures.

(iv)   ERT shall be familiar with Emergency and Evacuation Procedures as they apply in Administrative and/or Institutional Directives (a) 05.01.130 Escapes, (b) 05.01.120 Bomb Threat Procedure, and (c) 05.02.110 Fire Plan.

(v)   ERT shall ensure compliance with Administrative Directive (a) 04.04.102 Suicide Prevention and Intervention/Emergency Services. (b) Conducting wing tours at intervals of 30 minutes. Shall also ensure that the last two checks are being conducted during the first and last 15 minutes of each shift to sustain Residents' compliance with established regulations.

(vi) ERT shall also in the course of its duties, utilize the MMCall Tactile Paging System to provide notification to individuals in custody designated as Deaf or Hard of Hearing (HOH) who have been provided with a tactile pager. Any verbal announcement made to the housing unit such as yard lines, meal lines, weather emergency, etc. This information shall be sent as a group page to individuals-incustody provided with the tactile pagers. Additionally, individuals in custody may be individually paged for notifications such as med line, call pass, visit, etc. All staff shall equally be mindful that the system is for official purposes only. Informational pages shall be professional and respectfully worded.

(vii) ERT shall ensure all and any contraband discovered during tour of duty is processed according to Administrative Directive 05.01.112 Storage and Disposal of Contraband.

(viii) ERT shall ensure all movement of individuals in custody complies with direction set forth in Administrative Directive 05.03.106 Control of Individual in custody Movement.

(ix) ERT shall ensure DOC 0387 is completed along with an incident report. It shall provide this documentation to the facility Crisis Intervention

Team when individualsin-custody present signs of endangerment if not treated immediately.

Specific Responsibilities of ERT according to Facility Need(s): The list of specific responsibilities includes, but not limited to:

(i)   Assisting in responding to emergency codes within the work area

(ii) Assisting in moving or escorting Individual(s)-in-Custody designated as being placed on "Elevated Security status."

(iii) Assisting in the application of restraints with video-taping when Individuals-inCustody got ordered into 4-point Therapeutic restraints for mental health purposes.

(iv) Assisting in observing line movement to specific programming areas such as: yard, gym, group, etc.

(v)   Assist with conducting programming venue(s) and/or Classroom(s) checks when such are in sessions.

(vi) Conduct shake-downs as needed and in accordance with lay down procedures.

(vii) Ensuring all applicable and/or lay down guidelines are adhered to when strip searching Individuals-in-Custody.

(viii) Perform other duties as may be directed by the Shift Commander/DAO; Backup DAO and/or Chief Administrative Officer.

Chapter Six

6.0 Historical and Theoretical Perceptions of Mental Illness in the United States

Generally, Mental Illness is better referred as a broad range of disorders. These disorders may include sexual, eating, somatoform, anxiety and addiction disorders to mention but a few. And, despite tons of research on mental illness, much remains to unfold. Different professions have defined mental illness relatively different and, based on their peculiar fields and experiences with individuals who struggle with these disorders. However, certain variables are present in most and/or all the definitions and views. This is the fact that *mental illness* is a condition that affects a person's thinking, feeling, behavior or mood. According to Bible Society (2021 Ed.), mental illness is not a disease.

The article expressly stated: "Mental Illness is a behavior, not a disease." It also maintains that mental illness is a function of the mind and brain, which is embedded in moral conscious choices. It sustains the view as to why mental illness is not a body chemical or hormone related issues. That the etiology of joy and depression is a function of the mind and not the body. It also maintains that body chemicals and/or bodily dysfunctions do not cause choices. Whereas, human choices dictate human behavior, both good and bad. Examples of signs and symptoms of mental illness have been listed to include but not limited to: (i) Feeling sad or down; (ii) Confused thinking or reduced ability to concentrate; (iii) Excessive fear or worries, or extreme feelings of guilt; (iv) Extreme mood changes of highs and lows; (v) Withdrawal from friends and activities; (vi) Significant tiredness, low energy or problems sleeping; (vii) Detachment from reality (delusions), paranoia or hallucinations; (viii) Inability to cope with daily problems or stress; (ix) Trouble understanding and relating to situations and to people; (x) Problems with alcohol or drug use; (xi) Major changes in eating habits; (xii) Sex drive changes; (xiii) Excessive anger, hostility or violence; (xiv) Suicidal thinking or suicide ideation among others.

Mental Health America (2020) made contributions to this debate and argued differently regarding fundamental causes of mental illness. As stated in its submission, Mental Health America (2020) asserted that: "the brain is part of your body just like your legs or your heart." It went further in its analysis that: "Mental illnesses are brain-based conditions that affect thinking, emotions, and behaviors. Since we all have brains – having a mental health problem at some point during your life is common. Unlike other general physical illnesses, mental illnesses are related to problems that start in the brain. The brain is an organ. Just like any other organs in our body, it can experience changes (healing or injury) based on life experiences like stress, trauma, lack of sleep, and nutrition. Generally, when someone has a mental illness, something has changed in such a way that their brain and the way that it works has also changed. Mental illnesses can affect the rest of your body. Because of changes in physical activity sleep or other factors still being researched, people with mental illness are more likely to be at risk for other physical illnesses, like diabetes or pain. Ultimately it is important to remember that it's not one or the other, physical or mental, but that your whole body is interconnected. Therefore, taking a whole-body approach to getting healthier is so important. People who pay attention to their sleep, what they eat, or increasing exercise along with tackling negative moods and thoughts can reach greater improvements in their quality of life and their symptoms."

Historically, mental illness has been present throughout history of all ages. The evolution of mental illness, however, has not been linear or progressive but rather cyclical (Worthy; Lavigne and Romero, 2020). Whether a behavior is considered normal or abnormal depends on the context surrounding the behavior and thus changes as a function of a particular time and culture, Worthy; Lavigne and Romero (2020) stated. Overtime, ranges of theories and models have been employed to explain causes of mental illness. The theories include:

(i)   The General Theory: This theory was related to the predominant belief of the 20th century. During the 20th Century mental illness was ascribable to problematic relationships between children and their parents. This belief was held onto until the late 1990s. During this period, people believed child-parent relationship was a major determinant of severe mental illness, such as depression and schizophrenia.

(ii)   The supernatural theory of mental Illness. The theory postulates that individuals who suffer from mental illness are believed to be possessed by evil or demonic spirits. This may be as a result of displeasure of gods, eclipses, planetary gravitation, curses, and sin.

(iii)   The Somatogenic theory: This theory identifies disruption or interference in physical composition and/or physical functioning. This disturbance in physical operation is believed to be as a result of illnesses, genetic inheritance and/or brain damage or brain imbalance.

(iv)   The Psychogenic theory: the theory traces mental illness causes to trauma and/or stressful experiences. It also identifies malcognitions, or distorted perceptions to impact mental illness. In addition to these, etiological theories have expanded today to what the field of Psychology identified as biopsychosocial model to explaining human behavior in relation to social environment. This study postulates that socio-cultural factors such as sociopolitical or economic unrest, poor living conditions, trauma and/or problematic interpersonal relationships are contributory factors to certain inborn genetic predisposition which reflect in certain disorder.

This position maintains that certain psychological stressors need to be present for the development of the disorder.

(v)   The Medical Model Theory: This is also known as biomedical or disease model theory. This causative model theory focuses on hypothesized disease processes and symptoms which are said to be responsible for the associated disorder or disability.

(vi)   Biological Psychiatry Model: This focuses on organic or "hardware" pathology of the brain (*Wang, 2010*), where many mental disorders are conceptualized as disorders of brain circuits shaped by a complex-interplay of genetics and experience (*Murthy, et al. 2002*).

(vii)   Psychoanalytic theories: This theory puts attention on unresolved internal and relational conflicts. The theory is an upshot of 'biopsychosocial' model and it also relates to an eclectic mix of subtypes of psychoanalysis. These theories have been predicated as explanations of mental disorders. Many psychoanalytic groups are said to adhere to the 'biopsychosocial' model and to accept an eclectic mix of subtypes of psychoanalysis. Sigmund Freud developed the psychoanalytic theory. This theory of Psychoanalytic actually focuses on the impact of unconscious forces on human behavior. According to Sigmund Freud, the developer of Psychoanalytic theories, "a personality has three parts: the I.D, ego, and superego. The I.D operates under the pleasure principle, the ego operates under the reality principle, and the superego is the "conscience" which incorporates what is and what is not socially acceptable into a person's value system." This theory also specifies that there are five stages of psychosexual development that everyone goes through, these include: the oral stage, anal stage, phallic stage, latency stage, and genital stage. The theory asserted that mental disorders can be caused by an individual receiving too little or too much gratification in one of the psychosexual developmental stages. When this happens, the individual is said to be in that developmental stage. Hence, a disorder is a possibility *(Wang, 2010)*.

(viii) Attachment theory: attachment theory is a theory that focuses on the role of early caregiver-child relationships, responses to danger, and the search for a satisfying reproductive relationship in adulthood. The theory asserted that a child's attachment is to a nurturing adult. With the presence of this nurturing adult in the life of the child, the more likely that child will maintain healthy relationships with others in their life.

There are four patterns of attachment, according to John Bowl by who formulated the theory as contained in the strange Situation experiment which was demonstrated by Mary Ainsworth. These attachments include: secure attachment, avoidant attachment, disorganized attachment, and ambivalent attachment.

The attachments are equally said to be cross-culturally patterned. According to Wang (2010), later research found the fourth pattern of the attachments being referred to as disorganized disoriented attachment. Secure attachments however indicate trust in the child-caretaker relationship while insecure attachment indicates mistrust. In conclusion, the security (or the otherwise) of attachment in a child affects the child's emotional, cognitive, and social competence later in life.

(ix)   Evolutionary psychology (theory). This theory is also regarded as evolutionary psychiatry (theory), which posits that mental disorders involve the dysfunctional operation of mental modules adapted to ancestral physical or social environments but not necessarily to modern ones (*Wang, 2010)*. Behavioral abnormalities that resemble human mental illness have been found in related species such as in Apes. Relative assumptions suggest that mental illness could have evolutionary *advantages* for the species. These advantages might have included enhanced creativity and stress in a way towards enhancing survival through the activation of fight-response in anticipation of danger. Schizophrenia, delusion, Mania and depression have been included on the list of mental illnesses which might have been instituted by this evolutionary trail.

Accordingly, *Wang (2010) stated that:* "mania was set in motion during the spring and summer to facilitate energy for hunting; depression worked best during the winter, similar to how bears hibernate to recover their energy levels. This may also explain the connection between circadian genes and Bipolar Disorder and explain the relationship between light and seasonal affective disorder."

(x)   Genetics Theory: Through family linkage, some studies have continued to associate that genetic factors play major role in the evolution of mental disorders. Wang (2010) stated that: "The heritability of behavioral traits associated with a mental disorder may be in permissive than in restrictive environments, and susceptibility genes probably work through both "within-the-skin" (physiological) pathways and "outside-the-skin" (behavioral and social) pathways." Wang (2010) further stated that: "Research has shown that many conditions are polygenic in nature, which means that there are multiple defective genes rather than only one that is responsible for a disorder."

(xi)   Prenatal Damage Model: This relates to damages that occurred to a fetus while still in its mother's womb. This is considered to be a prenatal damage. Mental disorders can build in the course of pregnancy, if the pregnant mother uses alcohol or drugs. Also, if such pregnant mother is exposed to certain kind of illnesses or infections during pregnancy.

(xii)   Poor parenting, Abuse and Neglect Theory: Poor parenting theory has been largely associated with adverse childhood experiences. Such experiences may include physical or emotional neglect or both. It may also include: abuse, poverty and malnutrition. The developmental trauma resulting from such experiences may have long-lasting negative consequences on children. Research has shown also that several adverse childhood experiences can degenerate to certain level of stress known as toxic stress. As a result of such stress level, a child's neurological development can be disrupted when chronically exposed to stressful events such as physical, emotional, or sexual abuses; inclusive of, physical or emotional neglects. Poor Parenting or adverse childhood experience is clearly a risk factor for depression and anxiety. Lack of responsible parents, deprivation of required family socialization, lack of sense of belonging to proper family setting, family separation and/or unprecedented bereavement in families can be risk factors for psychosis and schizophrenia.

Referencing W.H.O (2001) reports, India, China and United States are the major countries mostly impacted by anxiety, schizophrenia, depression and bipolar disorder. According to available estimates in the reports, about 46.4% adults will experience a mental illness in the United States during their lifetime. About 5% under this category (18 or older) adults will experience a mental illness in any one year. This total sum up to, equivalent of 43.8 million people. Note, that there was no further available data to specify the demography of the above stated population within the country. Deidre (2016) published National Alliance data on Mental Illness to further buttress the above statistical enumeration when he stated in his analysis of "the 10 most depressed countries in the world" that, about one in five adults in the U.S. experiences some form of mental illness each year. He also asserted that only 41 percent of those affected received mental health care or services in the past years.

Chapter Seven

7.0 Review of IDOC Responsiveness to Mental Health-Treatment-Need within Its System

This section attempts to generate a list of significant measures taken by IDOC authority in response to peculiar Mental Health treatment needs of the growing population of mentally ill individuals within its system in meeting the "Rasho vs. Baldwin" settlement agreement. This list of significant areas of improvement includes:

(i)   Establishment of AD 404200 (Inpatient Mental Health) hospital with collaborative joint-management arrangement with Illinois Department of Human Service.

(ii)   Creation of Mental Health protocol manual and/or Standard Operating Procedure to enhance and establish direction and, to set guidelines for daily expectations towards sustaining improvement in service delivery.

(iii)   Creation of comprehensive Mental Health Quality Assurance Program.

(iv)   Improvement in cross disciplinary training programs to enhance mutual working understanding across mental health, medical, administrative and security employees.

(v)   Employment of more educationally enriched Correctional Employees referred to as Corrections Treatment Officers in place of regular Correctional Officer towards treatment improvement.

(vi)   Employment of more specialists such as Medical Doctors, Psychiatrists, Psychologists, QMHP, Correction Specialists, Leisure staff as well as Corrections Treatment Officers.

(vii)   Specific Treatment-focused programs for Individuals-in-custody identified as Serious Mentally Ill offenders.

(viii)   Improvement in timely reviews of personalized treatment plans.

(ix)   Establishment of improved and systematic screening program for individuals who present mental health symptoms upon intake and within both inter- and intrasystem transfers.

(x)   Establishment of appropriate Mental Health Levels of Care for need-based programming.

(xi)   Creation of multidisciplinary treatment options consistent with generally accepted mental health practices and in line with institutional requirements.

(xii)   Improved confidentiality in the process of medical and mental health record keeping and in view of accuracy and organized filling.

(xiii)   Improved suicide intervention services.

(xiv)   Creation of Treatment and Multidisciplinary Team Meetings for fact checks and, to ascertain accuracy in Treatment evaluation of the mentally Ill individuals.

(xv)   Deployment and improved focus on case management approach to treatment

(xvi)   Sustenance of psychotropic medication for Serious Mentally Ill Individuals during facility to facility transfers.

(xvii) Improved procedural approach in the usage of therapeutic restraints for mental health purposes.

(xviii) Significant reduction in unjustifiable use of force where adherence to crisis deescalation process becomes the emphatic preference of the department.

(xix)   Improved Suicide prevention measures.

(xx)   improved "Patient's engagement rate in Psychiatrist's evaluation as a result of S.O.P creation for daily accountability.

(xxi)   Improved monitoring against decompensation of Individual-in-custody in segregation unit.

(xxii) Improvement in Pharmacological treatment as well as counseling sessions of the mentally ill individuals-in-Custody.

(xxiii) Establishment of crisis intervention team.

(xxiv) Increased involvement of correctional staff in Crisis Training programs to improved knowledge shared across the different units involved in the process of Mental Health Treatment.

(xxv) Planned and/or work-in-progress approach in the area of Integrating Mental Health, Academic, Vocational, Leisure Times Services, etc. in the form of a Multidisciplinary Treatment Team approach.

(xxvi) Responsive review by MHP of cases of the Mentally Ill persons who get moved into administrative detention and/or segregation unit.

(xxvii) Improved documentation in the provision of structured out-of-cell time.

(xxviii) Improved documentation in the provision of unstructured out-of-cell time.

(xxix) Improved observation and follow-up calls' attendance on mentally Ill individuals in segregation unit.

(xxx) Improvement in documentation accuracy and effective usage of the offenders' disciplinary Tracking System.

(xxxi) Implementation of Review Committees for SMI individuals in segregation units in view of 60 days timely recommendation requirement.

(xxxii) Improvement in coordination and, growing MHP inputs in Adjustment Committee's dispositions and subsequent recommendations as it affects Seriously Mentally Ill individual(s)-in-Custody.

(xxxiii)   Improved cordiality between individual-in-custody and correctional staffs especially with the deployment of the use of less-aggressive pronounce such as: "Individuals-in-custody" while addressing incarcerated offenders.

Above listed areas of improvement are considerably least (as at the time of this compilation) compared to ongoing modalities, which the newly inpatient treatment facility is programming to launch and/or feature upon commencement of SMI treatment programs for committed persons in IDOC.

Chapter Eight

8.0 Samples of Reported Incidents: A Signal to Recidivism

In Review of the behavioral pattern of offenders classified as Seriously Mentally Ill persons who are currently enrolled in the mental health treatment programs within the department of corrections, a concerning pattern of behavior was noted as evolving. Many of these individuals-in-custody, behavioral (modifying) Patients, tend to intensify self-harming practices to achieve the following:

- To win medical determination to go to outside hospitals so as to be able to have access to comforting amenities, such as livestreaming television programs, cushion bedding and, to be able to have a feel of other exotic hospital facilities/environment.
- To be able to momentarily get away from prison-life and environment. And, to achieving the above, these individuals are willing to jeopardize their health in desperation to secure medical determination or order

to go to outside hospital. For this reason, any member of their body can be sacrificed in the process of self-harming.
-   To be able to mix-up and come around normal populace with regular life at the outside hospital.
-   Some male-offenders have also proven based on incidents that going to outside hospital is a way to spur their sexual urges where some of these individuals have inappropriately display their sexual organ to engage in masturbation upon sighting some of the female medical personnel who were assigned to care for them at the outside hospitals.

Candidly, this class of individuals-in-custody doesn't care about consequences of behavior. They act on impulse towards achieving the goal of winning attention without recourse for the cost of self butchering. As earlier stated, during staff responses to most episodes of self-harming within the BMU zone of the treatment center, the first statement from most individuals-in-custody classified as SMI has remained: "Take me to outside Hospital!" To enrich this knowledge, one of the mentally ill individual-in-custody had stated during one of his episodes: "I have 3 more months left here (in prison) with various inconclusive surgeries, how do you guys want me to survive if I get out this place?" This is the concern of this study; this is the part where correctional procedures for proper control and custody, towards sustaining safety and security of persons, cannot be jettison.

In other word, the laisser-faire advocacy will result in serious future complications for the system; it will clog the process of treatment and pressure diversion of resources (and possibly, diversion of attention). It will also retrogress the goal of corrections, re-exposed the vulnerability of the victims of crime and put the larger society in limbo of safety. Above is the least possible extent of recidivism where careful considerations and measures are not cautiously taken.

1st Sample of Reported Incident – Paraphrased (for privacy purposes):

NARRATIVE: Today, two zone supervisors were deployed to go to outside hospital to assist two Corrections Treatment Officers to de-escalate one of the Mentally Ill "Patients" who was refusing to leave the outside hospital facility after being discharged. "Patient" was actively threatening to self-harm when the two zone supervisors arrived at the hospital. "Patient" removed the IV from his arm and refusing to allow Hospital Medical staff to access the IV. After de-escalation attempts failed, the deployed supervisors gave the "Patient" four direct orders to comply but he refused to comply and continued to threaten to self-harm. At this point, "Patient" began to actively self-harm by attempting to pull his IV out, it took all the correctional staff present with combined effort from hospital security staff to place "Patient" into 4-pts restraints due to the selfharming behavior. "Patient' continued to agitate and remain combative. "Patient" bit the left wrist of the hospital security staff in the process of restraining him. At this point, one of the Zone supervisors administered a short-burst of foam oleoresin capsicum (pepper spray) into the "Patient's mucus membrane (facial area) to gain compliance. At this time "Patient" immediately complied and allowed the medical staff to properly remove the IV from his arm. "Patient' was then restrained for transportation back to the facility without issues.

DISPOSITION: Upon arriving at the facility, "Patient" was ordered into 4-pts restraints for Mental Health purposes by one of the MH Psychiatrists on duty. After medical assessment and cleansing for the effects of the oleoresin capsicum (pepper spray), "Patient" was secured in 4-point restraints without further issues.

2nd Sample of Reported Incident – Paraphrased (for privacy purposes):

NARRATIVE: Today Registered Nurse (RN) called shift commander and stated that (Facility Doctor) ordered one of the Mentally Ill *"Patients"* to go to the outside hospital for further testing. *"Patient"* has allegedly swallowed multiple items including his inhaler. *"Patient"* has been on a continuous watch for mental health purposes. *"Patient"* has been spitting out blood and due to the richness of the spit-coloration, medical staffs were unable to know the extent of his internal injuries, if any.

DISPOSITION: *"Patient"* was escorted to Outside Hospital for further treatment.

3rd Sample of Reported Incident – Paraphrased (for privacy purposes):

NARRATIVE: Today the wing Staff was conducting a wing check when the staff directly observed one of the Mentally Ill *"Patients"* engaging in self-harm and bleeding from the inner elbow area. The WingOfficer notified Zone supervisor who reported to the scene. *"Patient"* was placed in mechanical restraints and escorted to the triage area. Mental Health staff was notified, and a mental health assessment was completed. *"Patient"* was placed on a 10-minute crisis watch for mental health purposes and escorted to the dormitory where 4-point order was to be implemented. *"Patient"* claimed he used a piece of metal to self-harm.

DISPOSITION: Registered Nurse (RN) stated that the *"Patient"* had a 2-inch long cut in the inner crease of his left elbow and the nurse could not get the injured area to stop bleeding. Hence, Registered Nurse (RN) contacted Facility Medical Doctor for further direction. Resident's room was secured and sealed off for IA purposes due to the amount of blood loss. The facility Medical Doctor ordered *"Patient"* to be transported to outside hospital.

4th Sample of Reported Incident – Paraphrased (for privacy purposes):

NARRATIVE: Today Zone supervisor called the shift commander to report that he observed an open wound on one of the Mentally Ill *"Patients"*. The zone supervisor was intimated of this incident by one of the facility Behavioral Health Therapists (BHT) when the therapist saw the *"Patient"* actively cutting on his wrist in his room. When asked why he was self-harming, "Patient" stated that he was upset because he was removed from being on continuous watch. He added that he wanted to remain on continuous watch because he likes talking to people. *"Patient"* threatened to continue to self-harm if he was not placed on continuous watch.

DISPOSITION: *"Patient" received* treatment and he was placed into 4-point restraints for mental health purposes. Patient initially refused to go on 4-point but later complied after being de-escalated by correctional staff. The *"Patient"* was stripped searched to ensure he was not in possession of any additional instrument of self-harming.

5th Sample of Reported Incident – Paraphrased (for privacy purposes):

NARRATIVE: Today, one of the Mentally Ill *"Patients"* threatened to self-harm while speaking with a staff member. *"Patient"* pulled a piece of broken mirror from his genital area and began to cut himself. Zone supervisor gave *"Patient"* a direct order to stop but he refused and covered his room (window-view) with his mattress. Zone Supervisor opened his food port and moved the mattress from blocking the window-view only to find that the *"Patient" had cut on his eye-lid,* left eye. Zone supervisor gave *"Patient"* a direct order to stop and he refused, Zone supervisor dispersed a short burst of pepper spray. *"Patient"* then complied with security and was placed in mechanical restraints to be escorted to triage for assessment.

DISPOSITION: *"Patient"* was ordered into a 10minute crisis watch for mental health purposes per facility on-call Psychologist. Registered Nurse (RN) completed medical assessment on the *"Patient"* and he was secured in his room on 10-minute crisis watch.

6th Sample of Reported Incident – Paraphrased (for privacy purposes):

NARRATIVE: Today, Security officer reported this incident. The staff visually observed one of the Mentally Ill *"Patient"* ingesting what appeared to be a needle. Registered Nurse (RN) was notified who contacted on-call Facility Psychologist for further direction.

DISPOSITION: The On-Call Facility Psychologist ordered *"Patient"* to be placed into 4-point restraints for mental health purposes. Facility Medical Doctor provided additional instruction shortly after and ordered *"Patient" to* Outside Hospital for further necessary examinations.

7th Sample of Reported Incident – Paraphrased (for privacy purposes):

NARRATIVE: Today, one of the Mentally Ill *"Patients"* was directly observed engaging in self-injurious behavior by Security Officer. Officer contacted Zone supervisor and medical staff to report to the scene. *"Patient"* had generated a puddle due to the amount of blood found on the floor of his room.

DISPOSITION: ERT retrieved a piece of copper wire from the "Patient" and secured him into 4-point therapeutic restraints. *"Patient"* was also evaluated by medical staff and his injury was treated with gauze and tape while he remained secured in 4point.

8th Sample of Reported Incident – Paraphrased (for privacy purposes):

NARRATIVE: Today, a Qualified Mental Health Practitioner (QMHP) was completing crisis assessment and directly observed one of the Mentally Ill *"Patients"* using an eggshell to self-harm. *"Patient"* was cutting on his arms with the shell of an egg. *"Patient"* flushed the eggshell when staff asked to retrieve it. The reporting MH Practitioner notified the zone security supervisor and *"Patient"* was secured in restraints and escorted to the dayroom for medical and mental health assessment.

DISPOSITION: On-call MH Psychologist ordered *"Patient"* into 4-point restraints 10-minute crisis watch for mental health purposes. *"Patient"* was also seen and cleared by medical for superficial wounds. *"Patient"* was secured in crisis room without incident.

9th Sample of Reported Incident – Paraphrased (for privacy purposes):

NARRATIVE: Today, Zone Supervisor observed one of the Mentally Ill "Patients" engaging in self harm behavior inside his room. *"Patient"* was cutting on his left forearm with an unknown and unseen item. Zone Supervisor gave *"Patient"* a direct order to stop self-harming and *"Patient"* complied. Zone supervisor then gave "Patient" an order to cuff-up for medical assessment. "Patient" was placed on hand-restraint but he was reluctant to be escorted to treatment area. "Patient" attempted to head butt staff in the process of escorting him to treatment area. Both the zone supervisor and escorting correctional staff had to assist the "Patient" to the wall area to restrict him head-butting member of escort team. Zone supervisor's uniform and jacket were stained with Resident's blood in the process of escorting him to the wall to stop him assaulting staff by head butting. Medical and mental health staffs were notified of his attempted assault on staff.

DISPOSITION: RN assessed *"Patient's* wound and reported to the shift commander that the wound was approximately 1" long and 1/8" deep. Wound was cleansed and treated with pressure bandage. BHT conducted crisis assessment on *"Patient"* while MH Psychologist ordered "Patient" to go on 10minute crisis watch.

10th Sample of Reported Incident – Paraphrased (for privacy purposes):

NARRATIVE: Today, one of the Mentally Ill *"Patient"* was smearing feces all over the room and threatening to self-harm.

DISPOSITION: A QMHP completed a mental health assessment on *"Patient"* and spoke with the facility Psychologist who ordered *"Patient"* into 4-point restraints for mental health purposes. On-Call Facility medical doctor ordered "Patient" to outside hospital when additional information revealed "Patient" was throwing out blood, while also claiming he ingested unspecified number of acidic batteries.

11th Sample of Reported Incident – Paraphrased (for privacy purposes):

NARRATIVE: Today, one of the Mentally Ill *"Patients"* was directly observed by security staff banging his head against the wall. Staff notified Zone supervisor. Resident was placed in mechanical restraints and escorted to the dayroom for mental health and medical assessment.

DISPOSITION: MH Nurse Practitioner ordered *"Patient"* into 4-point restraints 10-minute crisis watch for mental health purposes after assessment.

12th Sample of Reported Incident – Paraphrased (for privacy purposes):

NARRATIVE: Today, Security staff was conducting a wing check when the employee sighted one of the Mentally Ill *"Patients"* utilizing a broken mirror to cut his left arm near his elbow. Staff notified control officer who notified the shift commander. Control Officer called Code 3 medical emergency. Other staff responded to the code, but *"Patient"* refused medical treatment and equally refused to sign the document indicating refusal of medical treatment. Registered Nurse generated an incident report advising of *"Patient"*'s refusal. Registered Nurse contacted on call Psychologist for further instruction.

DISPOSITION: *"Patient"* was placed into 4-point restraints for mental health purposes.

13th Sample of Reported Incident – Paraphrased (for privacy purposes):

NARRATIVE: Today, security staff was conducting Crisis Watch Check and observed one of the Mentally Ill *"Patients"* had climbed to the ceiling of Shower with both his arms extended. *"Patient"* damaged a sprinkler head and an access panel located in the ceiling of the shower. Security staff gave *"Patient"* direct order to come down and be placed into mechanical restraints which *"Patient"* complied.

DISPOSITION: Staff escorted *"Patient"* back to his room without further incident.

14th Sample of Reported Incident – Paraphrased (for privacy purposes):

NARRATIVE: Today, one of the Mentally Ill *"Patient'* had his* 10-minute 4-point crisis watch order discontinued by a mental health practitioner and the *"Patient"* was escorted back to his room by security staff. *"Patient"* was secured in his room but refused to give up the waist restraints to security staff through the food port. Several staff attempted to deescalate *"Patient"* at different times to gain compliance, but de-escalation was unsuccessful. Furthermore, *"Patient"* managed to disrobe and flip his restraints toward the front of him. *"Patient"* began to hit the room window-glass with the lock on his waist restraints to break the window. *"Patient"* was successful in his attempt to break the window and began to put the piece of glass in his mouth.

Staff gave *"Patient"* several direct orders to stop putting the pieces of glass in his mouth, he refused to comply. Zone Supervisor was called who also gave *"Patient"* direct order to remove the pieces of glass from his mouth. *"Patient"* spit the pieces out of his mouth and claimed he had swallowed a piece of it. Zone supervisor gave *"Patient"* direct order to turn around and allow security to re-secure the restraints on him to be able to remove him from the room. *"Patient"* complied and was escorted to dayroom for medical assessment.

DISPOSITION: On-call Psychologist ordered *"Patient"* into 4-point restraints on a continuous crisis watch. Medical Doctor ordered *"Patient"* to outside hospital for further medical examination due to the claims that he swallowed pieces of glass.

15th Sample of Reported Incident – Paraphrased (for privacy purposes):

NARRATIVE: Today, one of the Mentally Ill *"Patients"* stated to Registered Nurse that he has a needle on him and he was going to swallow it. Registered Nurse reported that she observed *"Patient"* swallowing what appeared to be an (IV) needle.

DISPOSITION: On call Medical Doctor ordered *"Patient"* to outside hospital.

16th Sample of Reported Incident – Paraphrased (for privacy purposes):

NARRATIVE: Security staff observed one of the Mentally Ill *"Patients"* had blood on his face and had engaged in self-harming on his eyes-lid. Zone supervisor was notified. Zone Supervisor reported and applied mechanical restraints on *"Patient"*. *Patient was* escorted to dayroom for medical assessment. *"Patient's* wounds to both eyes were assessed and cleansed.

DISPOSITION: On call Medical Doctor ordered *"Patient"* to outside hospital for further assessment upon being notified.

17th Sample of Reported Incident – Paraphrased (for privacy purposes):

NARRATIVE: Today, during mental health assessment session, one of the Mentally Ill *"Patients"* reported that he had swallowed unknown medication (pill) that he found on the floor. He also stated that he had inserted plastic into the injury on his arm. *"Patient"* refused medical assessment and treatment.

DISPOSITION: On Call Psychologist ordered *"Patient"* into 4-point therapeutic restraints for mental health purposes.

18th Sample of Reported Incident – Paraphrased (for privacy purposes):

NARRATIVE: Today, one of the Mentally Ill *"Patients"* was assessed by a QMHP who reported that "Patient" had engaged in self-harming behavior and threatened to continue throughout the evening. The QMHP notified Zone Supervisor who notified on call Psychologist.

DISPOSITION: *"Patient"* was ordered into 4-point therapeutic restraints after medical treatment to his wounds.

19th Sample of Reported Incident – Paraphrased (for privacy purposes):

NARRATIVE: Today, security staff was conducting wing-check when one of the Mentally Ill *"Patients"* notified the employee that he had self-harmed by cutting his testicles open. *"Patient"* was escorted to triage via wheelchair by Zone Supervisor and ERT.

DISPOSITION: Facility Medical Doctor was contacted and *"Patient"* was ordered to be escorted to outside hospital after in-house medical assessment.

20th Sample of Reported Incident – Paraphrased (for privacy purposes):

NARRATIVE: Today, Registered Nurse (RN) was conducting medication pass in the Dormitory when she observed one of the Mentally Ill *"Patients"* swallowing half of a stapler remover instrument. *"Patient"* immediately began to cough out blood.

DISPOSITION: On call medical doctor ordered *"Patient"* to be escorted to outside hospital via state vehicle.

21st Sample of Reported Incident – Paraphrased (for privacy purposes):

NARRATIVE: Today, the Continuous Watch Officer stated that one of the Mentally Ill *"Patients"* had smeared feces on his window glass and placed mattress against the window to block his room-view. "Patient" also remained non-compliant to deescalation attempts. Upon arriving at the scene, the zone supervisor sighted *"Patient"* with a piece of string around his neck. "Patient" had also cut on his inner left arm and above his left eye at this time. Security staff was able to successfully grab and cut the ligature from the "Patient's neck, utilizing a knife for Life. *"Patient"* was placed in handcuffs and escorted to dayroom for medical assessment.

DISPOSITION: On-duty RN assessed "Patient" while a MH Nurse Practitioner ordered "Patient" to be placed in 4-point therapeutic restraints for mental health purposes. ERT team escorted the "Patient" to implement the 4-point order after being searched.

22nd Sample of Reported Incident – Paraphrased (for privacy purposes):

NARRATIVE: Today, a security supervisor was conducting round when he sighted one of the Mentally Ill *"Patients"* laying on the floor of his room with a ligature tied around his neck from a piece of his safety smock. Upon gaining entrance into his room, unsuccessful attempt was made to remove the ligature from around his neck. At this time, a Code 3 (Medical Emergency) was called. A knife for life was obtained and utilized to cut off the ligature. *"Patient"* was placed in handcuffs and escorted to dayroom for medical assessment.

DISPOSITION: Both RN and MH staff conducted assessments on *"Patient."* "Patient" was properly searched and secured in 4-point therapeutic restraints by ERT.

23rd Sample of Reported Incident – Paraphrased (for privacy purposes):

NARRATIVE: Today, security staff during wing check observed one of the Mentally Ill *"Patients"* hitting his head against the wall and refused direct orders to stop until his head started to bleed. Zone supervisor reported to the scene and contacted the on-call MH Psychologist.

DISPOSITION: On-call Psychologist ordered *"Patient"* to be placed on 4-point 10-minute crisis watch for mental health purposes. *"Patient"* was properly searched, offered a safety smock and secured in 4-point therapeutic restraints by ERT team without issues.

24th Sample of Reported Incident – Paraphrased (for privacy purposes):

NARRATIVE: Today, during wing-check, one of the Mentally Ill *"Patients"* informed security staff that he had inserted an object into his eyes. Attending security staff personally observed blood streaming from his lens area. Zone supervisor was notified who called for "Patient" to be medically assessed. *"Patient"* stated to Nursing staff that he had inserted staples into both of his eyes. *"Patient"* was placed in handcuffs and escorted to holding area for medical assessment. *"Patient"* was then taken to triage to be further evaluated.

DISPOSITION: Facility Medical Doctor ordered *"Patient" to* be escorted to outside Hospital.

25th Sample of Reported Incident – Paraphrased (for privacy purposes):

NARRATIVE: Today, one of the Mentally Ill "Patients" during security wing check called the attention of Zone supervisor and stated that he needed help. *"Patient"* was initially standing near the door without his safety smock on and then stepped back to be in full view of the supervisor. At this time, the supervisor was able to see that "Patient" had a piece of green string tightly wrapped around his genitals. "Patient" was ordered to put his safety smock on. He complied to have handcuffs applied on him. *"Patient"* was escorted to the holding area for both medical and mental health assessment.

DISPOSITION: Upon assessment, "Patient" was ordered to go in 4-point for mental health purposes by the ordering MH Psychologist.

26th Sample of Reported Incident – Paraphrased (for privacy purposes):

NARRATIVE: Today, security staff called Code 3 (medical emergency) due to observed activity of one of the Mentally Ill "Patient" self-harming by opening his chest cavity with his institutional identification card.

DISPOSITION: As a result of the extensive self-harm to the chest, the facility medical Doctor recommended "Patient" to be escorted to outside hospital via emergency services.

27th Sample of Reported Incident – Paraphrased (for privacy purposes):

NARRATIVE: Today, during wing check, security staff directly observed one of the Mentally Ill "Patients" ingesting multiple pills and cutting on his inner right arm with a piece of medallion. Zone supervisor called medical for assessment. "Patient" refused medical assessment. "Patient" also refused to give up the piece of medallion he was utilizing to self-harm. After continuing de-escalation attempts, supervisor was able to place the "Patient" in handcuffs and escorted to dayroom for medical assessment.

DISPOSITION: Facility MH Psychologist initially ordered "Patient" to be placed in 4-point. But, upon being contacted, the on-call medical doctor made determination to order "Patient" to be escorted to outside Hospital for further medical examination.

28th Sample of Reported Incident – Paraphrased (for privacy purposes):

NARRATIVE: Today, one of the Mentally Ill "Patients" inserted a foreign object inside his Penis. "Patient" stated that he inserted a piece of seg-pen inside his penis.

DISPOSITION: Security staff completed mental health assessment on the "Patient" and contacted on-call facility medical doctor who ordered "Patient" to be transported to outside hospital.

29th Sample of Reported Incident – Paraphrased (for privacy purposes):

NARRATIVE: Today, one of the Mentally Ill "Patients" swallowed one arm of his eyes-glasses during med-pass. "Patient" began to throw out blood.

DISPOSITION: Attending Registered Nurse (RN) staff reported to facility Medical Doctor who ordered "Patient" to be escorted to outside hospital via state vehicle for further examination.

30th Sample of Reported Incident – Paraphrased (for privacy purposes):

NARRATIVE: Today, one of the mentally ill "Patients" grabbed a supervisor's shirt through the food-port while standing by the front of the "Patient's room. The "Patient began yanking the shirt to cause bodily harm. It required the combined effort of other security staff to get the supervisor's shirt off the grip. **DISPOSITION:** The shift Commander was notified. Mental Health Unit was equally notified. Mental Health Assessment was conducted. Patient was secured back in his room thereafter without further incident.

31st Sample of Reported Incident – Paraphrased (for privacy purposes):

NARRATIVE: Today, one of the mentally ill "Patients" swallowed an unknown object attached to a string that was hanging from his mouth. "Patient" started throwing up during this episode. Zone supervisor called the attention of the medical unit. Attending Nurse observed that there was blood in the vomits of the "Patient."

DISPOSITION: Attending Registered Nurse (RN) contacted the on-call Medical Doctor. The Facility Medical Doctor ordered "Patient" to be escorted to outside hospital via state vehicle for further medical examination.

32nd Sample of Reported Incident – Paraphrased (for privacy purposes):

NARRATIVE: Today, one of the Mentally Ill "Patient" self-reported that he had inserted two flexible segregation pens into his urethra. Zone supervisor notified MHP of this information. MH staff conducted assessment on the "Patient."

DISPOSITION: MH authority ordered "Patient" to go on 10-minutes crisis watch for mental health purposes. Upon being contacted, the facility medical doctor ordered "Patient" to be escorted to Outside Hospital for further medical examination.

33rd Sample of Reported Incident – Paraphrased (for privacy purposes):

NARRATIVE: Today, during med-pass, security staff and Registered Nurse directly observed one of the Mentally ill "Patients" swallowing a 2-inch long piece of wire shaped into a hook. "Patient" was placed in handcuffs for his own safety and, he complied to be escorted to dayroom for medical evaluation.

DISPOSITION: Attending Registered Nurse (RN) contacted the on-call medical doctor who ordered "Patient" to be escorted to outside hospital for further medical examination.

34ᵗʰ Sample of Reported Incident – Paraphrased (for privacy purposes):

NARRATIVE: Today, security staff called code 3 when the employee observed one of the Mentally Ill "Patients" rolled up his bed sheet, tying the sheet around his neck and trying to choke himself. Zone supervisor gave the "Patient" 3 direct orders to stop choking himself, but "Patient" refused to stop. Zone supervisor released a short burst of Oleoresin Capsicum (Pepper Spray) to stop the "Patient" from attempting to choke himself. The "Patient" stopped, and security staff gained entrance into his room to secure him in mechanical restraints. "Patient" was escorted to dayroom for medical assessment.

DISPOSITION: "Patient" was offered and refused shower. Attending Registered Nurse (RN) cleansed his face for decontamination from the effect of Oleoresin Capsicum (Pepper Spray) and medical examined him. No injury was reported. Behavioral Health Therapist (BHT) conducted behavioral assessment on "Patient" and MH Psychiatrist ordered "Patient" to go on continuous watch upon reassessment. Shakedown procedure was completed and Medical walked the wing to ensure other residents were not affected by the effects of the Oleoresin Capsicum (Pepper Spray). No injury was reported by staff except minor irritation from the effects of Oleoresin Capsicum.

35th Sample of Reported Incident – Paraphrased (for privacy purposes):

NARRATIVE: Today, one of the mentally ill "Patients" cut on his eyelid with a small piece of razor blade. MH Psychiatrist was contacted who ordered "Patient" to go on 4-point therapeutic restraints. Upon being advised to comply with the 4point order, "Patient" refused. After several failed de-escalation effort, ERT was activated.

DISPOSITION: ERT leader gave the "Patient" one direct order and "Patient" complied to be handcuff and escorted to 4-point room without issues. After completion of room and body searches in line with extant procedures, "Patient" was secured into 4point therapeutic restraints for mental health purposes without further incident.

36th Sample of Reported Incident – Paraphrased (for privacy purposes):

NARRATIVE: Today, Zone supervisor found one of the Mentally Ill "Patients" in pool of blood in his room due to self-harming activities. Zone supervisor notified the shift commander. Medical staffs were directed to 10-25 the location. Upon being medically assessed, attending medical staff discovered that "Patient" could not talk for a moment due to swallowing unknown object as well. Upon regaining his voice, "Patient" stated he swallowed half-side of a staple removal instrument, which he initially selfharmed with. "Patient" was coughing out blood profusely. His vital signs were checked and found to be within the normal range.

DISPOSITION: Registered Nurse contacted on-call Medical Doctor who ordered "Patient" to be escorted to outside hospital via state vehicle.

37th Sample of Reported Incident – Paraphrased (for privacy purposes):

NARRATIVE: Today, Zone supervisor notified shift commander that one of the Mentally Ill "Patients" informed the supervisor during wing check that he self-harmed by inserting five triple AAA batteries and a piece of wire approximately three to four inches in length into his urethra. Attending RN conducted medical evaluation and reported findings to on-call medical doctor.

DISPOSITION: The Facility Medical Doctor made determination for "Patient" to be escorted to outside hospital by state vehicle for further examination.

38th Sample of Reported Incident – Paraphrased (for privacy purposes):

NARRATIVE: Today, staff notified zone supervisor that he observed one of the Mentally Ill "Patients" during wing check self-harming. Zone supervisor reported to the scene and saw "Patient" with a laceration, which was measured to be 3/4 inch in length and 1/4 inch in depth to his left inner elbow with a piece of broken mirror. Zone supervisor gave "Patient" multi direct orders to stop self-harming, but "Patient" refused. Resident informed zone supervisor that he would comply if he was provided a wheelchair because he was unable to stand due to swallowing a nail clipper and three AAA batteries.

DISPOSITION: A wheelchair was fetched. "Patient" complied upon sighting the wheelchair while he continued to clamor for hospital need. "Patient" was escorted to dayroom and was medically evaluated by on-duty Registered Nurse (RN). "Patient" was secured in a dry cell for close monitoring due to his claims of swallowing nail clippers and three batteries. Facility Psychologist also directed for the "Patient" to remain on continuous mental health crisis watch for mental health purposes. "Patient" was to be reassessed later by a representative of the mental health department.

39th Sample of Reported Incident – Paraphrased (for privacy purposes):

NARRATIVE: Today, one of the Mentally Ill "Patients" inserted a piece of broken comb inside his penis. "Patient" also refused to come out of his room for medical assessment.

DISPOSITION: Attending RN notified Facility Medical Doctor who ordered "Patient" to be escorted to outside hospital by state vehicle. "Patient" however continued to refuse medical assistance. After a session of deescalating effort, "Patient" complied and was escorted to outside hospital via state vehicle.

40th Sample of Reported Incident – Paraphrased (for privacy purposes):

NARRATIVE: Today, during evening medication pass one of the Mentally Ill "Patients" self-reported to Registered Nurse that he was bleeding from his rectum.

DISPOSITION: Attending Registered Nurse (RN) reviewed his medical information and viewed his previous x-rays which verified that "Patient" had a yet-to-be extracted foreign object in his rectum due to previous self-injurious behavior. On-Call Facility Medical Doctor was contacted who ordered "Patient" to be escorted to outside hospital via state vehicle.

41st Sample of Reported Incident – Paraphrased (for privacy purposes):

NARRATIVE: Today, one of the Mentally Ill "Patients" inserted a foreign object inside his penis. Resident self-reported that he inserted a piece of plastic inside his penis. "Patient" was unable to urinate and required medical assistance.

DISPOSITION: Security staff completed mental health assessment on "Patient" and availed the Oncall Medical Doctor the findings. The Facility Medical Doctor ordered "Patient" to be escorted to outside hospital via state vehicle.

42nd Sample of Reported Incident – Paraphrased (for privacy purposes):

NARRATIVE: Today, staff directly observed one of the Mentally Ill "Patients" laying in pool of blood and appearing to be unconscious. A code 3 (Medical Emergency) was called. "Patient" had cut on his inner left elbow using piecesof a broken mirror. Responding security staff assisted "Patient" to his feet, confiscated the pieces of broken mirror and escorted him to triage for medical assessment.

DISPOSITION: On-Duty Registered Nurse (RN) wiped the blood stains off the "Patient's body and medically evaluated him. Upon completion of assessment, MH Psychiatrist ordered "Patient" into 4-point 10 minutes crisis watches for mental health purposes. "Patient" was secured into 4-point without further incident.

Chapter Nine

9.0 Mental Health Crisis De-Escalation: A Shift in Approach & Practice

(Power-Point Template on the Lecture Delivered by Stephen B. Oladipo, PhD – Jan 2021)

MENTAL HEALTH:

CRISIS DE-ESCALATION
(A shift in Approach & Practice)

Introductory Puzzle

What need or purpose does 'Crisis de-escalation' serve if we are already prepared to slam the food-passage and throw in the food tray – avoiding the least possible contact with the Resident?

First Message

If we cannot get the perception right, we can never be able to get the approach right.

Getting the Right Definition Right

You need to know that:

- A Resident is NOT one of your colleagues
- A Resident is not your subordinate
- The Residents are not your enemies or oppositions

THE RESIDENTS ARE YOUR PATIENTS

WHO IS A PATIENT?

- A Patient is someone who is at Risk

- A Patient is someone who is sick

- …someone who is unstable.

- A Patient is someone who does not have his/her faculties together (Mentally speaking)

- Someone who cannot holistically account for his actions

- Your Patients are not normal. If they are normal, they will not be in custody. (And guess what happens if they are not here? It simply means, there is no treatment-job for you & I).

- A Patient is someone who needs help and

- A Patient is someone who is under care.

Let's Face the Fact

- Often than not, the situation we find ourselves as correctional staff who are assigned and deployed to look after these patients stems from our first approach when we had contact with the Patients. Like the saying goes: "The first approach matters most."

- As personnel, you have a patient who is already agitated before you meet him/her and when you look up this guy's record; this was a Patient who possibly: committed murder to get his sentence; beat up a peace officer to get into prison or committed one violent act or the other to being where he is. How then do you think approaching such a person with a baton in your hand, with an OC in your pocket or a mean-looking-face will be the intimidating tools you need to submit such a personality?

- If you walk down your wing upon resumption of duty without proper perception of whom your patient is and this patient hurt you with the **'right'** insult, do you get to flow at the same level and threaten such "Patient" with all the instruments of punishment that are available and at your disposal? OR, do you just look at this "Patient" and remind him with a smile that YOU ARE ONLY HERE BECAUSE YOU WANT TO ASSIST HIM? This is the point where most crisis situation builds up once the right approach and the right perception become missing between a Patient and an employee when it matters. But, with the right perception of whom this patient is when he upsets your spirit at the start of your shift; a crisis and a TACT-TEAM situation may be avoided for that day.

WHAT YOU MUST AVOID IN YOUR FIRST CONTACT WITH YOUR PATIENT

- Don't confront your Patient with a posture that suggests contrary intentions to your de-escalation approach.

- Never start up your day with a look or attitude that suggests: 'it is WE against YOU or We are ready for you."

- Do not go to your Patient with an attitude that reveals "I can write you up," "We can put you on restraints," "We have powers to secure you."

  Please hide those instruments the Patient already knows you possess them.

CONTINUATION

- If your Patient ever gets in troubles and need to go on restraints or be controlled into compliance; never show signs of WINNER or LOSSER towards him/her. Rather, be sober for him/her.

DESIRABLE TOOLS TO SUCCESS

- **Attitude**: Never bring your personal or domestic struggles to work, it will complicate things for everyone. Be conscious that the entire facility can be in turmoil just because you fail to show up at work with a pleasant spirit & a light mood. Hence, you must build an attitude to see crisis de-escalation as a serious business that starts with your action & in action.

- **Interest**: Crisis De-escalation wouldn't just take place with a casual effort or 'I don't care disposition.' You have to be interested in imbibing by the rules guiding the process of de-escalation. Empathy can enhance your interest.

DESIRABLE TOOLS TO SUCCESS CONT.

- **Passion**: This is where it concerns you. Remember, having disowned all your official punitive tools for your de-escalation effort to be effective; the only POWER you want to resort to is your PASSION. Why? Because the real meaning of power is regarded as: 'ability to influence the behavior of others without resistance (using variety of tactics to push or prompt their action)." This therefore relies on how you see yourself on the job. How you see yourself as a professional. Are you planning to be a successful counselor in later years in your career, this is a good skill-development field for you. Or if you ever wish to influence someone positively in life, you can test your success rate here or build up your skills from here. Summarily, be passionate about what you do, it makes the difference.

DESIRABLE TOOLS TO SUCCESS CONT.

- **Call for help/Teamwork:** Sometimes, someone else already built some sort of influence or rapport with that Resident or Patient, it makes the job easier. Don't do it alone; call such colleague to help you chat the "Patient" up, it preserves time. Remember this is not a glory-taking adventure but a team-work effort. Let the most effective staff for that situation handles the problem. And, never divide your ranks because the same Resident(s) can see it.

KEYNOTE

The bane of this approach is to prepare your mind and admonish you so you don't get the steps wrong towards crisis de-escalation which is the only way we all can close the day in a win – win situation. Also, it appears the best option for everyone in any given working day.

MUTUAL RESPECT

- Everyone responds to respect no matter how mad. Be consistent with RESPECT, it will pay off.
- You can never be a successful crisis deescalator without 'purpose-driven' respect.
- Be aware that inmates are first HUMAN before being convicted...please respect their HUMAN dignity even when their 'rights' don't cover for it.
- Never trade 'tit' for 'tat,' often than not, it is more difficult to correct an error by initiating another error. Stay with Respect even when the Patient doesn't respond to it.

THE GOAL

Remember the primary goal of crisis deescalation (aside being professional on duty) is to be able to have a nice day at work and go home safe. If all reasons fail why you feel it is unnecessary to be nice; keep this at the back of your mind that your individual attitude can cost everyone else the troubles running around to deal with another crisis situation. Hence, let's play our own individual roles well to avoid escalating situation which can be avoided with our willingness to see the Residents in the right definition of whom they are: "PATIENTS."

The Final Word:
CONSISTENCY

CONSISTENCY IS ABILITY TO SELF-MOTIVATE IN FRONT OF FAILURE.

Note that this approach will not work in all situation and at all times but with your resolve to be consistent seeing the Residents in the right context of whom they are; which is, as your Patients and, with the willingness to follow through some of the recommendations on proper response to Patients' insults and excesses; the facility will experience more crisis-free days where staff can be more comfortable coming to work and going home safe.

Chapter Ten

10.0 Monthly Supervisory Training Memos – Bothering on Safety & Security (Researched & Delivered by Stephen B. Oladipo, PhD)

Training #1: Safety and Security Sustenance

Safety and security are important terms that are associated with the protection of a person, organization, and property against external threats that are likely to cause harm. The need for safety and security is about measures to guarantee a safe environment. This also means that safety comes first before other needs or expectations can be met.

Note that without proper security of our environment, safety is definitely in doubt. But as security employees we cannot compromise proper security of the facility, which, in turn, guaranteed everyone can go home safe.

Sub-Topic: Need for Effective System Check

System checks are not limited to those exercises we do when a supervisor takes your equipment and demand for incident report because you noticed it. System checks are concurrent, reoccurring and, they are those constant observations and attention you pay to your security environment to ensure nothing is missing, nothing is falling, nothing is unusual and everything is properly functional. This is suffice to say, system checks are daily, hourly and continuum while working in any penitentiary environment like ours. We cannot avoid doing proper and effective system checks because our own safety as staff is first dependent on it. While conducting a system check however, items to examine on a security check should include:

1) Structural items, such as: (a) Locks and keys (b) Fasteners and hardware, such as screws, bolts, and hinges (c) Doors, windows, windowpanes, frames, and bars (d) Inside walls, outside walls, mortar joints, ceilings, and floors (e) Utility systems, such as: Drains, utility access doors and panels, Air vents and ducts.

2) Lighting, light fixtures, and electrical outlets and cords.

3) Perimeter security checks: Our perimeter visual inspection shall be routine and random (That is: no less than once per day). This check should include: Inspection of outside walls against damage, tampering or other indications of attempts to breach security. (ii) There should be no person(s) loitering in adjacent parking areas or otherwise acting in a suspicious manner. (iii) Look for Potential security problems related to design, construction or maintenance. (iv)

Check out the Perimeter lighting and the surveillance systems from time to time.

4) Our Fire and safety hazards equipment are equally parts of our important checks. This is one of the reasons we do fire drills so we can check out these equipment and be sure they are not rusty.

5) Last, but not the least, sanitation of the facility. Without proper sanitation, we will by ourselves create health-hazard. Remember, this is where we spend most hours of our days as employees. Failure to keep the facility clean will expose us as employees to health hazards. Hence, proper sanitation enhances safety while the primary purpose of security is to attain safety.

Training #2: Back to Basics security 101: Staff and Facility Safety

Be advised that basic security starts and ends on the safety of staff as well as the Residents.

Sub-Topic: Shakedown of Residents' Living Areas

Shakedown is the search of the entire facility or major area(s) within the facility. It may also be a search of designated housing unit(s).

The Purpose of this shakedown training include:

(i)   to enhance our muzzle memory towards conducting regularly the required random shakedown of Residents' living areas;

(ii)   to remind us of the need to prevent contrabands within our system;

(iii)   to reinvigorate the procedure for thorough search of the Residents' living areas as well as all ports of supply entrances into the facility.

As a reminder, the directives surrounding facility searches are detailed in our post descriptions as supervisors. Residents are equally familiarized with this process through their orientation handbook. Some searches are expected to be conducted at irregularly timed period while some are occasioned as immediate security situation demands.

Note: Only contraband items should be confiscated during shakedown and not Residents' allowable property except if such property is distorted from its original form.

Necessary Items for effective shakedown: Items that may be needful for result oriented shakedown include: (i) flashlight (ii) probing tools (iii) Evidence tags &bags (iv) metal detector (v) flexible mirrors (vi) metal picks/magnets etc.

Training #3: Audit

Sub-Topic: Importance of Security Audit

Audit is the inspection of various books of records by an auditor in addition to physical checking of inventory to ensure all units or departments are in tandem with proper documentation procedures and established recording system for proper accountability of all tools and equipment towards enhancing safety and security of the institution. In other words, auditing is conducted to confirm compliance and to ascertain the accuracy of data inputs or records provided by the institution or facility.

Types of security audit include: (i) compliance audit, (ii) vulnerability assessment, (iii) risk assessment and (iv) penetration testing.

Objectives of security audit:

(i)   To assess the effectiveness and efficiency of security measures and their compliance with Government Security Policy (GSP) and Operational Standards.

(ii)   To ensure adaptation to or regularization of existing procedures prior to any major system or procedural changes, modification or adjustment.

(iii)   To ensure enhanced security through such process of regular threat and risk assessments conduct.

Benefits of Security Audit:

(i)   To help identify security loopholes

(ii) To track effectiveness of security policy or strategies

(iii) To assist employees or security staff stick to security build-up practices and Standard Operating Procedures and,

(iv) To enhance the process of new policy formulation.

Guidelines to conducting effective security audit include:

(i)   Effective planning

(ii)   Be articulate about your plan and strategies.

(iii) Understanding the objects and subjects of your audit

(iv)   Know what or whom your contacts are

(v)   Have access to relevant or relative information

(vi)   Have access to relevant resources.

(vii) Specify details as best possible.

(viii) Assign scores where and when necessary

(ix)   Note areas of compliance

(x)   Identify areas of default or lapses (for improvement call)

(xi)   Be time conscious and endeavor to meet your deadlines.

Training #4: Basic Security Expectations

To be efficient in our responsibilities as security supervisors, the first thing we need to be aware of is to be knowledgeable of the risks and dangers our laxity can cause the institution. Therefore, our knowledge and training should help us adapt to the dynamics and incessant changes going on in our institution (e.g. Staffing Constraints, and/or emphasis on minimal use of force). Tools availability: DRT, strategic approaches and other crisis deescalation-skills that lay demands on our individual expertise towards ensuring we deliver a safe & wellsecured treatment center in a penitentiary institution.

Sub-Topic: Custody, Control and No-Disorder

Custody: Under basic definition, custody is the retention, safe-guarding, and securing of a thing or person. Note however that custody is core in any and every correctional facility's responsibilities. We must keep these individuals and we must keep them safely.

Control: *Generally, security controls* are measures to avoid or minimize security risks. Please be advised that the entire facility is under our operational jurisdiction as correctional employees. Any contraband found within the facility is directly exposing our laxity. We must take charge of the environment and assume full responsibility. The Residents are under the control of our institutional policies and procedures. This is why the Resident cannot dictate to us. The Residents cannot hold us helpless. We have the responsibility to be a step ahead in our thinking and strategies. We must be on top of the situation at all times.

No-Disorder: As more and more restrictions are relaxed and daily activities are beginning to open on all shifts (after the covid-19 siege), disorderliness cannot be tolerated. Nevertheless, the ways to avoid disorderliness are through concurrent planning and effective coordination. And, as a team, we need to be speaking in the same language. We need to be moving in the same direction. We need to be able to show one-front before the Residents. We cannot allow the Residents to perceive the animosity between us as individuals. This is the only way to be successful and to avoid frequent disorderliness in our routine activities and in our line-movements.

Training #5: Post Description & Responsibilities

On a broader term, post descriptions can be viewed as a 'group of duties and responsibilities', which require the services of an employee. Better still, it can be branded as a statement which outlines the specificity of a particular job *or* position.

Sub-Topic: CTOS Post Descriptions: A Review & Reminder

Basically, a CTOS post description is a carefully designed written packet which detailed the job specifications of a Corrections Treatment Officer Supervisor in line with the ADs and IDs of the institution and Department.

What does this mean?

This means that as a CTOS who voluntarily accepted to serve in this position and capacity; you can be held responsible for failing to perform some and all of these functions (extractions from CTOS Post Description packet):

(a) You are directly responsible to ensure you attend monthly staff meetings…and present any unusual problems that you have encountered in carrying out your assigned duties.

(b) Directly responsible to conduct security inspections on a regular basis for purposes of controlling contraband and detecting any breach in security. JTC is divided into unique working zones as outlined in I.D

05.01.110…The zones include: Both Daily and Weekly categorization for inspections.

(c) Directly responsible to perform gallery checks at a minimum of twice per shift. You must sign in the wing log each time the gallery check is conducted.

(d) Directly responsible to ensure staff remains at their assigned location(s)…and duty posts.

(e) Complete all necessary reports pertaining to residents, tools, equipment, inspections, and any incidents, and forward same to proper authorities.

(f) Directly responsible to be present and available to help direct CTO(s) on proper procedures and policies.

(g) Shall ensure all toxic and hazardous materials are used and stored in accordance with Administrative Directive 05.02.115 Toxic Substance.

(h) Directly responsible to performing all other duties as required and / or assigned.

Above is the reason it becomes imperative to familiarize yourself as a CTOS with all and most of these job details so that you do not claim ignorance of your responsibilities. Remember, 'ignorance of the law is inexcusable.' Please let's get more familiar with post description and job assignment towards proficiency and productivity enhancement.

Training #6: Security Supervision

Sub-Topic: Effective Supervision of Line staff

Supervision is the act of supervising, directing, guiding or overseeing the day-to-day work activities of the line staff in every organization and establishment; especially more in a correctional institution like ours. The role of supervision may sound simple but in practice, it has been observed to be more involving especially within every and all correctional institution(s). The role and the reason for supervision must be clearly marked out as we set out every day to provide leadership and direction to line staff. This is important because if we fail to deploy effective supervision, the goal, the mission and the program of the institution may be negatively impacted. It is also important to understand as supervisors that: the department of correction believes we will deploy effective supervision, this is why we are graced with higher authority above the line-staff and, this is also why the pay-checks look better.

Part A: What does effective supervision involve?

(a) to effectively guide the line-staff towards appropriately performing their functions and assignment in line with provisional policies.

(b) to effectively provide direction and leadership by example.

(c) to effectively ensure that staff remain on their assigned posts and operate strictly in accordance to post description.

(d) It also involves the responsibility to inform staff-violators of policy and procedures (Like a policing duty).

(e) Effective supervision upholds and sustains discipline within the ranks.

(f) Importantly more, an effective supervisor serves as an advocate for his line-staff and helps them navigate daily issues regarding work responsibilities, colleague-issues and person(s)-served issues.

Part B: What Effective supervision is NOT?

(a) Effective supervision is NOT an opportunity to create division (divide and rule) among your personnel or line-staff.

(b) Effective supervision is NOT an opportunity to harass or bully your line staff.

(c) Effective supervision is NOT an opportunity to utilize state's apportioned authority to gain personal popularity (the good-man syndrome) for self by way of over-looking staff's excesses while they are violating departmental rules and procedures.

(d) Effective supervision is equally NOT about competition with colleagues for staff's likeness. Rather, effective supervision is more about your exhibition and deployment of fairness and equity across board in the performance of daily duties.

Training #7: In Time of Disturbance

Disturbing moments are bound to arise at one point or the other in the course of provision of daily services with the individuals-in-custody. Needless to state that situation of disturbances are frequent occurrences in the Behavioral Management Unit of the institution.

Sub-Topic: Reactionary gap and Secured Environment: Ways to Mitigate Staff Assaults

A safe and secure environment is one in which all element of insecurity is taken into consideration at all times and importantly, before venturing into a scene of incident to reduce the likelihood of unknown assault. Cultivating this procedural habit of considering the totality of circumstance will always help to safeguard us from assaults and injuries.

What is a reactionary gap? A 'reactionary gap' is the distance between the extremities of your reach and the extremities of your opponent's reach... their reach includes any weapons they may have! More elaborately defined, a reactionary gap is the distance between you and an "unarmed" — or not visibly armed — subject in an "unusual" environment. Most defensive tactics systems teach that you should be between six and eight feet from the subject with your hands up in a good bladed stance.

Informative Signals to prompt your initiation of 'reactionary gap': (a) When Resident's behavior appears to be odd (b) When his movement towards you appears questionable (c) When you are aware the Resident is in sharp disagreement with your instruction (d) When the Resident refused your direct order and verbally challenge you (e) When his outward appearance suggests he is up to something (f) If he has had issues or tensed argument with you in recent past (g) If you perceive he is luring you into a circumstance or position that will limit your reactionary tendencies; initiate a reactionary gap.

Factors that inclusively influenced staff assaults are identified to include: (a) Location of incident (b) Shift of Occurrence (c) Officer's workexperience (d) sex (gender) of the officer (e) Age of the person-in-custody (f) Total number of staff present at the scene (g) Total number of Resident(s) present at the scene

Statistical account on Staff Assaults: How often are correctional officers assaulted?: - A 2015 study in the U.S. concluded that for every 10,000 full-time Correctional Officers, there were 254 workplace assaults and violent injuries reported in 2011 that's 36 times the rate for all American workers (NCBI, 2021).

Why is a reactionary gap important?:

Reactionary gap is important to allow you the time to react if the subject becomes violent and makes move to attacking you.

As supervisors, how do you reduce staff assaults and properly secure your environment?:

1. Stick to your Policies and Procedures

2. Be aware of who is present, close-by or at reachable range during Resident Disturbance and at all times.

3. Be aware of what is present: Instrument and tools.

4. Be aware of your numbers against your Residents' numbers (Before you react or resort to immediate use of force).

5. Be conscious of reinforcement (reinforcement could be either way if you have Residents with accessibility to reinforcement prior to your own reinforcement arrive – don't let this happen to you).

6. What's your "End Point Security" (E.g. On a night shift if we lose some sort of control, do we have secured end point security – i.e. the security control system within the facility. This may also refer to the effectiveness of programmed backup system, if any?).

7. Identity and Access Management (IAM) - what kinds of security set up or access do we deploy as a facility? (Soft-Ware based (Multi-Factor Authentication (MFA) OR key control)? You know the answer. Let that guide your module-operandi. How effective is our facility's key-control set-up, operationally?

Training #8: Mental Health Emergencies

Sub-Topic: Crisis Mitigation & Suicide Prevention: The roles of Treatment Officers

A mental health emergency is a life-threatening situation in which an individual is imminently threatening harm to self or others; severely disorientated or out of touch with reality; has a severe inability to function, or is otherwise distraught and out of control.

A mental health crisis is when an individual in custody feels he is at breaking point and he needs urgent help. Some of the symptoms include: (i) feeling extremely anxious and having panic attacks or flashbacks; (ii) Feeling suicidal or self-harming.

(A) What are the roles of Treatment Officers in situation of mental Health Emergencies. The roles include: (i) to mitigate crisis and (ii) to Prevent suicide attempt(s);

(B) How do Treatment Officers effectively fulfill these roles: Treatment officers can effectively fulfill these roles of crisis mitigation & suicide prevention through: (i) following procedural details (post descriptions); (ii) ensuring complete and genuine crisis assessment and (ii) through doing due diligence when being assigned as:

- Continuous Watch Officer
- Suicide (10 Min.) Watch Officer
- Close-Supervision (15 Min.) Watch Officer and/or,
- Periodic (30 Min.) Watch Officer.

Training #9: Heightened security and Staff Preparedness

Heightened security can be defined as a mindset that leads you to notice unusual or suspicious behavior or circumstances and, reporting your observations to authorities in a logical, rational and timely manner. It is not intended to induce fear and/or panic.

Sub-Topic: Duty-Staff Posture in a Security-Related work-environment

The definition of our posture as correctional treatment staff working in a penitentiary environment was one of the basic knowledge disseminated at the Correctional Training School where every correctional staff graduated from. The first principle was the need for staff to be at alert at all times. Hence, security posture is a measure of: The level of visibility you have into your watchsurrounding and into any and every potential attack (assault) point(s). These also include the controls and processes you have in place to safeguard yourself and others within the potential assaultradius. Your level of alertness simply redefines your ability to detect and contain attacks/assaults. This also relates to your ability to be able to promptly react to and recover from such attack or workrelated assault (s).

In recent time, the kind of attitude, posture, utterances, and disposition, which staff exhibit (in the notice) of the Individuals-in-custody is clearly empowering the Residents to believe they can run our security setting /staff over and deploy complexity to confuse the management. It is important therefore to note that once we have come to that point where we have lost our state-accorded authority to perform the basic function of CUSTODY and CONTROL, then we are sending the wrong signal out that we are in a wrong profession. Be mindful therefore that Criminal Justice Profession is a profession that is self-introductory; meaning that our job-functions, as correctional staff, revolves around people who are criminal minded, people who are unlawful-in-behavior and equally unruly. Then having this at the back of our minds, how do we get to duty-post and suddenly expecting everything to be smooth-riding and prompt obedience from the people we serve? Again, this is what defines us as correctional staff. The training, the skills and the ability to control and keep the Residents in shape as well as in line with correctional regulation and ordinances, those are the commitments we affirmed to. We may indeed struggle with this at first but, until the Residents begin to understand these expectations before their terms are served and conform to orderliness. That is the basic assignment in our hands as trained employees of the department.

Never forget this, and always remember that Security means safety, as well as the measures taken to be safe or well secured.

Training #10: Security Watches and Visibility

Security and visibility are Siamese twins in any and every security setting. One cannot successfully operate without the other. There can be no safety or security without visibility. In other words, both safety and security are in doubt where visibility is in doubt.

Sub-Topic: Operational Visibility in a Security Environment

As a term, visibility is a measure of the distance at which an object or light can be clearly discerned. By this provision, clear visibility may require a good ambient light: artificial or natural day light. Hence, there can be no visibility without well lighted environment. This goes to mean that wherever you notice a faulty light feature, please never fail to file in a work order.

By literal definition, Visibility is the ability to have an unobstructed view of the object under surveillance or ability to see and to be seen especially in a secured environment.

In security, visibility goes both ways:

(i)   First, it applies to how well you are able to see your object of security. That is the individual-in-custody whom you are trying to secure or be in control of. This is because your ability to have a full glance of this individual can dictate how safe you can be and, as well as how safe and secured this individual can also be.

(ii)   Second, visibility also applies to ability for you to be seen (by security cameras and/or colleagues) at all times in the course of performing your duties. Some of the dangerous examples we have had in the time past have included situations where female staff have gone into MaleResidents' rooms all by themselves without the awareness of both the control officer(s) and/or the supervisor(s). There is no better way to explain how dangerous this kind of behavior is and, how expensive it can cost us both as individual(s) and as an institution. Please, never trivialize visibility.

Of importance is the need to understand equally that certain things are not visible to the naked eye, but that doesn't mean they are invisible. And, our ability to notice these things and proactively advance measures to mitigate such issues is key. For instance, Residents' behavioral attitude, verbal/reactionary messages and perceived gangling among Individuals-in-Custody. These are issues that may latter develop to pressuring the security deployment if we fail to notice them in the course of our watch-duties.

(A) Why is visibility important? Conscious Visibility enables us to identify problems before they erupt into larger issues. This includes noticing a nail on the walkway and refusing to pick it up. That nail may get into a wrong hand latter and cost the institution an emergency hospital furlough. This may also include ability to sight a reaction and be able to address it proactively before it reaches a level of crisis or escalated concern.

Again, it cannot be over-emphasized that; the overall goal of having a clear view of our watchenvironment is primarily for safety. And, in every work environment like correctional institution, safety is paramount. Hence, visibility is indispensable to the continuity of safety and security of both staff and Residents.

Training #11: Civility

Civility simply means formal politeness and courtesy in behavior or speech. Whereas, Politeness is the practical application of good manners or etiquette so as not to offend others. Civility also comes from the Latin word *'civilis'*, meaning "relating to public life, befitting a citizen." In other word, Civility is a polite act or a polite expression.

What does lack of civility means? It means: Incivility. Incivility is verbal or nonverbal communicative behavior indicating disrespect for another person, compromising the cooperative action necessary for human communities to flourish. Incivility is a general term for social behavior lacking in civility or good manners. This ranges from rudeness to lack of respect for elders, to disobedience and hooliganism. The word "incivility" is derived from the Latin incivilis, meaning "not of a citizen"

Sub-Topic: Civility, Respect and Authority to succeed in Supervisory Obligations

Please be advised that there is a huge correlation between Respect and the authority you command in your workplace as a supervisor. Remember, civility means politeness. But before you can gain politeness, respect for one another comes along. This suffices to mean, if you lose a portion of your personal respect to someone, you have invariably lost a portion of your authority to influence the behavior of that person, especially in a work-related environment. Hence, if we continue to accumulate and tolerate disrespectful behaviors in our work environment, we are simply raising a community of uncivilized personnel. The fault will not be on the staff, the blame simply comes to us the supervisory cadre.

Respect, they say, is reciprocal and, it must also be heralded in our day-to-day operation. There must be decent respect between a supervisor and a supervisee. We also have a need to respect our Resident-population because they are human like us. We have a need to respect their choices first. We can invoke our procedural policies thereafter by following due process to sustain control. That's in situation where those choices infringe on the procedural regulations of the institution. But respecting the Residents' choices come first to deter us from liability of excessive use of force towards sustaining control as custodians.

Your symbol of authority emerges first from the adornment of the "White shirt" but the "white shirt" has no authority on its own other than the one that the individual who adorns such "white-shirt" attracts to it. Also, note that Authority is what your presence commands anywhere you show up within the facility as supervisors. The logic is, If we have been showing up and our presence means nothing to those who are abusing departmental directives; then it simply means we have depreciated in our authority and there is no way we can be able to successfully fulfill our core mandates of supervision without authority.

As a supervisor, If you have to stand with your subordinate every minute on your shift to argue and debate why you want them to do what the institution directed them to do, then, we are fast depreciating in our authority and we will be ineffective in the performance of our functions.

What then is the goal of civility?

(i)   the goal of civility training is to help employees develop a sense of respect for others in the workplace.

(ii)   to teach employees about self-awareness, integrity, ethics, communication, and interpersonal skills.

Characteristics of civility:

• Mutual respect.
• Respect for the rights of others.
• Recognizing and respecting the dignity of others.
• Dignity and dignified behavior.
• Belief in the inherent good of other colleagues & subordinates.
• Giving others the benefit of the doubt.
• Respect for privacy.
• Respect for right to be left alone (when such is demanded).
• Adherent to policy and procedures which you sign for as well as your work ethics.

Last but not the least, taking the High Road: – This means perseverance & endurance during tough times (Tough times come to us all in the course of life and in the process of our career development even with balancing personal/family life against career demands. Imbibing attributes of Civility will help us significantly).

5 Ways to Promote Civility in the Workplace:

1. Pay Attention: Note that simply being observant and considerate can go a long way toward making others feel valued and appreciated.

2. Acknowledge Other People. Recognize their input and performance.

3. Be Inclusive. No man knows it all in life. Hence, share with others what knowledge you have and add to your knowledge from their own shared experience.

4. Respect other people's space.
   Also, be Respectful of Others' Time. If we must accomplish a joint task, please don't say: "I will do it at my time. There should always be a "we" and not a "me or I" spirit among us.

Training #12: Integrity

Integrity is doing the right thing even when no one is watching. In other word, Integrity is the practice of being honest and showing a consistent and uncompromising adherence to strong moral and ethical principles and values. In ethics, "integrity is regarded as the honesty and truthfulness or accuracy of one's actions." (Free source: Wikipedia)

Sub-Topic: Work environment &Integrity in Service Delivery

Why is workplace integrity important?

Workplace integrity is important because: Integrity at work encourages positive work culture. Every responsive service-delivered is accompanied by uncompromised integrity. According to Random House Dictionary, integrity is: adherence to moral and ethical principles; soundness of moral character; soundness in judgment and, honesty. When we look around us in the course of performing our duties, we want to ask, are there replica of these attributes within our facility and in what we do as individual? If your answer is unclear, then, you have a conscious personal duty to perform. There may be a need to retune ourselves as individual so that we can be able to recreate our work environment, which will in turn reflect in our service delivery. When trust is lack, it becomes extremely difficult to work with one another and this will create a work environment that is totally unacceptable to the Department as an agency of the state. This is why the department of correction keeps probing into incidents and circumstances of unethical practices within the work-environment. Because without these checks and balances, lack of integrity will ruin every goal and mission of the agency.

Note that: Anyone can deliver a service, but; no service is considered excellent without integrity in the delivery of the service. Without integrity: values, trust, and the image we projected as an institution will depreciate. Lack of integrity utterly brings distrust. While existence of integrity disperses corruption and shrouded practices.

How to Demonstrate Integrity in Service Delivery:

- Always thrive to tell the truth
- Don't Abuse your position (Power-drunk; flamboyancy; Complacency; Men-pleaser Attitude can engender position-abuse)
- Be prompt to accord others the respect they deserve
- Try collaboration rather than competition
- Thrive to meet your deadlines
- Uphold moral standards and,
- Approach challenges with courage

To Sustain Your Work Integrity means:

- You are trustworthy and reliable
- You encourage open and honest communication only among your peers
- You learn to be responsible for your actions

Training #13: Teamwork in Security Environment

- If safety is indeed our watchword as correctional employees, then, working as a team in a volatile environment is not an option. Divided we fall and united we stand. According to Bang Gae, "Teamwork makes the dreams work." Robert Orben also added a voice to the importance of teamwork when he stated: "If you can laugh together, you can work together." And, Jean-Francois Cope admonished that we should build "teamwork over personal ambition."

By way of definition therefore, teamwork is the collaborative effort of a group to achieve a common goal. Teaming is the synergy that enhances capacity to achieve more with combined effort. It has been said that talent only wins a game, but it takes a team to win a championship. If we continue to work together as a team, it has been said, we will eventually develop an increased level of bonding. Note however that envy, acrimony, and animosity will only destroy a team and leave each member worse off than they started off. It has also been said that there is strength in oneness while division exposes our individual weaknesses.

Defined differently, a team, is a group of interdependent individuals who work together towards a common goal. Teaming is also the ability to work with others and to help others attain their full potential. H.E. Luccock highlights the importance of teamwork when he constructed this statement: "No one can whistle a symphony. It takes a whole orchestra to play it."

There are three major key characteristics of a team, these include: (i) shared goal (ii) interdependence and (iii) boundedness. Other characteristics of teamwork include: (i) harmony, (ii) partnership (iii) synergy (iv) unity (v) alliance (vi) assistance (vii) coalition and (viii) confederacy.

To be successfully built as a team, we must sustain the following attributes. These attributes include:

(i)   Open communication to avoid conflicts.
(ii)   Effective coordination to avoid confusion and the overstepping of boundaries.
(iii)   Efficient cooperation, especially in the form of workload sharing.
(iv)   High levels of interdependence to sustain high levels of trust
(v)   Mutual support and cohesion.

Note that if the team spirit is strong and genuine, our output and improved efficiency will attest to it.

The process of bonding in group-building includes the following stages: (i) Forming: This describes the process of coming together; (ii) Storming: this characterized the process of competition for power & authority. This is the stage in every team where ability to manage conflict becomes imperative to be able to hold the team members together. This is the stage they need the knowledge and education to know they can only engage in healthy competition and not rivalry; (iii) Norming: At this third stage, successful management of the second stage will result in solidary-building, interdependency, and cohesiveness among the team members; (iv) Performing: this final stage builds on everything that the past stages have built up. Once positive, a peaceful co-existing environment will begin to exist towards high level performance, productivity, and efficiency in matured interdependency.

Finally, note that a sustainable teamwork environment will without doubt enhance the spirit of togetherness and engender a problem-solving culture through multi-participatory approach. Such environment will accord each team member the opportunity to make contributions and have their opinions count. On the overall, continuity in teamwork will result in gainful decisions that will be beneficial to every member and the core mission of the department. Hence, there is no alternative to teamwork in any demanding and safety-requiring work-area.

Training #14: Ethical Standards

Ethic can be defined as the moral code that guides the behavior of employees with respect to what is right and wrong in relation to conduct and decision making. It is also the moral principles that govern a person's behavior or the conduct of an activity. Better still, ethic is the branch of knowledge that deals with moral principles.

To say this as it should be, our core function as supervisors centers around our ability to uphold the ethical standards of the organization. This also implies that we need to lead by example. Like the saying goes, to whom much is given, much is expected. If we can't up our ethical standards, we will lack the moral justification to correct others.

Examples of ethical behavioral expectations of the department from us include:

(i)   Sustenance of our Grooming standards
(ii)   Complete and Correct Dressing with the right gears
(iii)   Professional conduct
(iv)   Objectivity-approach to official matters
(v)   Sustenance of values and respect for authority.

We have a duty to remind ourselves of the above from time to time. We also have a duty to continue to thrive to keep up with these expectations. Thriving to achieving ethical standard is the hub of professionalism. Hence, the attitude we display towards the above subject-matter defines our measure with professionalism.

Training #15: Performance Evaluation & Feedback

Performance evaluation is the process of reviewing the effectiveness of employees or how successfully the employees are fulfilling their job's responsibilities in contribution to the overall organizational goals. Defined differently, performance evaluation can be regarded as employees' appraisal. Ideally, performance evaluation should be periodic and systematic. It should take into cognizance a regular documentation of activities, contributions and/or attitude to work. This also includes employees' performance in relation to time management; punctuality; record of absenteeism and other form of performance-enhancing skills, which an employee exhibits or fail to exhibit towards fulfilling his/her job expectations.

Why do we conduct performance evaluation?

(i)   To enable the organization gathers the right information about best way to approach attaining its sets of institutional goals.

(ii)   To enable the organization understands how employees view organizational processes and procedures.

(iii) To enable the organization understands the right approach to help or assist employees towards fulfilling their individual roles or job responsibilities. Many organizational policies and practices are also evaluated in the course of this process especially through the impact of such policies on performance.

(iv)   To enable the organization to understand recurring challenges in the field and how to ameliorate such challenges. For instance, to determine where training, development and/or motivational programs are needed. And it also helps to assess whether these have been effective.

(v)   To enable the organization to know which employee(s) are more dedicated to job-responsibilities and how to further encourage such employees to do more.

(vi)   To afford the organization the knowledge about which employee(s) struggles with performing their roles and to know why and importantly,

(vii) To engender needed feedback towards overall organizational goals' enhancement.

Feedback is a critical part of performance evaluation process. Feedback enhances understanding of what is lacking, what is not and what must be added; either in terms of training or resource-input towards achieving the desire results. Feedback is however a dual process: (a) from employee(s) to supervisor and/or (b) from supervisor to employee(s). The challenging aspect of feedback is usually from supervisor to employee(s) because the process can produce strong reaction. Nevertheless, engendering feedback is very critical to the effectiveness of performance evaluation process.

Basic Assessment during Performance Evaluation includes:

(i) Self-Assessment and
(ii) Supervisor's Assessment

Examples of Specific Areas of employees' performance evaluation include:

(i)   Attendance Evaluation
(ii) Training and improvement
(iii) Workload or output measurement
(iv) Attitude to Job-Responsibilities
(v)   Attitude to Rules and Regulations etc.

Expectations (behavior vs result):

To appraise performance effectively, supervisors must:

(i)   be aware of the specific expectations (post descriptions),
(ii) monitor the employee's behavior and results,
(iii) compare the observed behavior and results to expectations and
(iv) measure the match between them.

Training #16: Effective Supervision of Line-Staff

Supervision is an act of supervising, an act of overseeing and of giving direction to subordinates. One of the critical positions to attain in the course of career is supervision. Supervision goes with accountability, objectivity, responsiveness, professionalism and directional-ism. You cannot disassociate those tenets or core-values from supervision. You also cannot hand-pick some of the core-values and leave the others. Nevertheless, when we fail to equip ourselves genuinely with these core-values, our area of assignment, our position responsibilities and the high-expectations on us as individuals and position-holders are disappointed.

As supervisors, we need to:

(a) Engage and

(b) Redirect.

It is upon us to fulfill all of these expectations and justify the essence of our position rather than disappointing it. As supervisors, we have to engage our staff positively and effectively and we have to effectively redirect them towards accomplishing the required post-descriptions.

Hence, be mindful that you can never be an effective supervisor If you ever get to a point in your career where you lack the effrontery to redirect and positively engage your line staff, especially those who are directly under the purview of your direction.

Elements of Effective supervision:

(i)   Clarifying the purpose of assignments.

(ii)   Providing detailed directions and instructions.

(iii)   Working with the staff to completing the assigned tasks.

(iv)   Regular review of work-assignment.

(v)   Make your engagement a learning opportunity for staff.

(vi)   Clarify expectations

(vii)   Demonstrate your own willingness or dedication to work.

Training #17: Supervisory Roles & Due Diligence

By definition; due diligence is the reasonable steps taken by a person in order to satisfy a lawful requirement or established procedure. In other words, due diligence is the careful, reasonable and necessary measures exercised by someone to ensure assigned roles are effectively implemented and/or performed. This implies that; to be effective in our roles as supervisors, we must inculcate due diligence in the performance of our functions.

Be aware that the essence of supervision is to ensure your supervisees are well guided, properly directed and you clearly understand that supervisory roles demand effective performance of oversight functions in reviewing the activities of your supervisees. This also goes to explain how sincere evaluation of an employee is conducted during performance reviews. Ideally, these reviews are not meant to be copy and paste but an objective submission free of parochial sentiments and politicking.

By standards, areas of reviews may include: affirmative attendance, attitude to work, responsiveness to assignments and/or deployment, problematism, willingness to help or assist in other areas (additional duties); ethical positioning on the job among other factors.

The core principles of due diligence include the need to be:

a. **Firm**: let your subordinates know that your response to impropriety yesterday is still the same response you have for the same behavior today. Separate yourself from the slogan that "if you can't beat them, you join them." That is not a good trait of a resolute leader. Stand your grounds for good and be defined by what you stand for. Exhibit potentials that reestablish your leadership capability.

b. **Fair**: You must be fair to all as best as you can. You may not be perfect but thrive towards fairness.

c. **Consistent**: Do not be the type who changes the goalpost in the middle of the match. Let your consistency define you as an individual. Showing undue preferences in critical situation where your leadership capability is put to test will ruin your ability to build a personality for yourself. This clearly deals with objectivity, knowing as a leader you cannot take sides unfairly. You will lose the trust which your subordinates repose on you.

Hence, doing due diligence on duty post includes properly conducting an assignment given to you. For instance, if you are directed to conduct uniform inspection at roll call, don't just tick the document without actually assessing the staff. It is in the performance of this role that you can help the staff to know the exact expectations of the organization as regards to dressing.

Chapter Eleven

11.0 Ten (10) Principles to Guide Staff-To-Patients' Relationship in IDOC Treatment Centers - An Addendum:

1. IDOC Treatment centers are not typical correctional facilities, but Mental Health Treatment Centers; let this purpose of establishment guide your conduct – always!

2. The clients here are called Patients/Residents. This implies they are not 100% healthy (mentally or otherwise). Please, treat them with that in mind. You are not in position to assess who is faking it. MPH experts will get that figured out.

3. Note again that, if these Patients are normal or have their behavioral attitude in order, they will not be here for treatment. And,

4. If the Patients are not here, THERE WILL BE NO EMPLOYMENT-VACANCY FOR YOU & I under this IDOC treatment program with promising career path and good pay-check.

5. Be guided that the treatment facility is not a law court where an offender faces judgment for his/her wrongdoing. Remember, the Patients here have already been through that Sentencing trail-path previously. Hence, stop engaging in judgmental practices against the individuals-in-custody.

6. Staff to Patients relation should never be: 'Commander vs. Subjects" kind of relationship. Rather, Patients should be acknowledged as people with series of mental health deficiencies. Hence, the whole essence of staffing is to be able to support them in every way possible in the course of treatment.

7. Be aware that majority of the Patients are already victims of anti-social issues, having been estranged from the etiquettes of relationship with the larger society to say the least. Hence, building a professional friendliness-environment will be a paid-assistance any staff can render.

8. Always remember that the clients are your Patients, not your colleagues. Hence, do not try to get even with them on reactionary terms.

9. It is a necessary requirement to unbundle your loads of personal problems if you must function effectively in your roles as a treatment personnel within the IDOC Treatment Center.

10. You can only be an agent of change and positive influence when you see your job beyond the 'paychecks.'

THESE PRINCIPLES WILL LEAD YOUR WAY TO SUCCESS IF YOU TRULY ACCEPT YOUR POSITION AS YOUR PATH TO CAREER-FULFILMENT!

Chapter Twelve

12.0 Security and MH Procedural Checklist for Staff Working with Mentally Ill Offenders

1. Is the vicinity lit up and well ventilated?
2. Are the tools and/or equipment well organized and available for quick access? (Such as: Knife-for-life, spit-hoods, cuffs, pepper spray, flex cuffs)
3. Is the room-temperature within the normal range
4. Was the water monitoring procedure observed?
5. Are the food-ports effective and in good working order and, can easily be secured?
6. Are the doors and closets secured firmly?
7. Are proper restraints procedures followed prior to exiting individuals-in-Custody from their rooms and back?
8. Are these individuals pat-searched before and after movement?
9. Is movement in compliance with in-house movement policy and procedures?
10. Is movement properly documented and authorized?

11. Are there regular and random searches of offenders' living areas?

12. Are vacant rooms properly searched prior to occupancy by new "Patients"?

13. Is there search of common utility-areas such as showers prior to offenders' entry?

14. Is there proper documentation such as a log for Residents' grooming services e.g fingernail cuts?

15. Is there a functional schedule for such grooming activities?

16. Are rooms, doors and windows clear and unobstructed?

17. Are the wing checks regular and timely?

18. Are all logs being completed in a timely manner?

19. Are individuals-in-custody with appropriate property (property compliance) without excess luggage to create nuisance?

20. Are the rooms clean and orderly?

21. Does staff know what key go into what door?

22. Do exit areas have clearly designated signals?

23. Does staff know the emergency room entry and exit procedures?

24. Is the facility evacuation procedure known to all staff?

25. Does staff have easy access to the evacuation procedural templates for fire or natural disaster?

26. Is there a known procedure staff can follow when "Patients" take food-ports and refuse to give them up?

27. Does staff apply their uniform gears (e.g., duty belts) properly for easy hosting of operational equipment such as Pepper sprays, keys and cuffs?

28. Does staff adhere to 'out-of-room' schedule or procedures for individuals-in-custody especially regarding interviewing with MHP?

29. Is the location for the out of room time and interviews searched prior to "Patients" entering the area?

30. Is the time used for interview and out of room session properly documented?

31. Is there a log for all activities including Mental Health interviews?

32. Does Mental Health staff sign in and out every time they enter and/or leave interview session?

33. Is the interview area open and accessible for proper monitoring by security staff?

34. Can privacy be maintained and sustained based on designated area of interview?

35. Are the doors to the interview section closed and gave room for privacy while interview is in session?

36. Is the offender being searched before and after interviews with Mental Health staff?

37. Is there space or demarcation between Mental Health staff and the offender during interviews?

38. Is the interview room free of clutter or unused objects?

39. Is there proper security set up to monitor interview room and identify risks and/or attend to concern from Mental Health staff?

40. Were all applicable doors secured at all times (e.g., cell house, gallery entrance)?

41. Was officer positioning safe while applying restraints?

42. Was proper application of restraints re-checked prior to moving "Patients"?

43. Was the Escort Officer properly position during escort?

44. Are light fixtures working properly without defaults?

45. Are cell doors, windows, and walls free of coverings?

46. Is the tool or cleaning equipment room secure?

47. Are inventories issued accurately and documentarily, correct?

48. Is work order submitted for any observed maintenance issue such as: cracked glass, malfunctioning food ports, plumbing defaults etc.)?

49. Is there a procedure to review the logs against Maintenance database?

50. Does staff know what each key on their assigned key ring is for or where it accesses?

51. Are staff knowledgeable of their assigned duties and responsibilities while on their respective posts?

52. Is staff familiar with the use of SCBAs and fire suppression equipment?

53. Does staff adhere to escort procedure?

54. Prior to departing the work-area, does staff conduct proper pat-search using metal detector on offenders who work in areas where critical tools are utilized and/ or where hazardous contents are deployed?

55. During line movement, do lines paired up in columns of two while moving Residents?

56. Do random pat-searches take place during major line movement(s)?

Chapter Thirteen

13.0 Recommendations

In wrapping up this engaging and inexhaustible study on effective management of mental illness without widening recidivism in contemporary correctional setting, advancing the following recommendations become necessary:

(1) It is imperative for state(s) and local authorities within the communities to encourage and deploy government mechanism to re-institutionalize the family system where values and process of socialization can be sustained. Since record indicates that the larger percentage of individuals-in-custody enlisted for MH treatment programs are predominantly young males and females who grew up without balanced or proper family socialization. Strong family reinstitutionalization campaign is a key recommendation of this study and, this is believed to have potentials to re-write current concentration of young adults in jails and/or in Mental Health centers.

(2) There is a need to explore alternative to incarceration in 21st century America. Since the overwhelming analysis on the effect of incarceration has gravitated towards how offenders in US have come to accept the prison life as a new world to build their own socialization and subculture to avoid the innate ability to be responsible for themselves in the capitalist world. The acceptance of Prison life is directly influencing the increasing figures of prisoners and, the push to identify as offenders with mental illness issues. National Institute of Justice corroborated this fact as reported by World Population Review thus: "…almost 44% of criminals released return before the end of their first year out of prison. In 2005, about 68% of 405,000 prisoners that were released were arrested for a new crime within three years, and 77% were arrested within five years." The number of people who will reengage with the criminal justice system highlights the critical importance (…) of reentry (Martin and Garcia, 2022).

(3) Strong collaboration between the court and correctional administrators to enhance understanding of the court in relation to operational challenges within the corrections and, to enhance performance measurement data exchanges in continuous reviews of developments regarding mental illness treatment within the correctional system is very imperative.

(4) The need for participatory review of treatment measures by all stakeholders within the criminal justice system is of essence to ensure proper dimension(s) to

full deployment of mental health treatment program within a penitentiary environment in a manner that such programming does not jeopardize the primary goals of corrections.

(5) Continuous measurement and adjustment must be made and be prepared for, where and when such adjustments are necessary in the course of time and/or through the phases of program-implementation and, through the course of push and pull feedbacks.

(6) There should be an establishment of program review unit within the treatment center. This review unit should be saddled with responsibility to gather data through reports and on-site incidents; accumulate and analyze such data or reports to detect behavioral patterns and, to measure improvement or deterioration of programming effects on the overall. This assignment is deemed necessary to enhance projection, amendment to strategies and to aid recommendations for improved decisions. The above recommendation is important because the Individuals-in-Custody for whom the program is designed will continue to explore possible loopholes to their advantage and, towards making the treatment strategies ineffective.

(7) Federal authority should earmark special fund and make provisions to enable state agents develop programs to ease transitioning from prison to community much easier to reduce recidivism.

(8) Ranging from: Discharge/Release planning approach, which is a process of creating a continuum of care

after incarceration; to Critical time intervention style, which is a treatment model of transitional support from correctional setting into the community; to Case management interventions and/or Intensive community treatments respectively; these programming designs and models must be fully deployed and approached on a need-based basis to be able to effectively address recidivism at community reintegration level to sustain successful re-entries.

(9) Stakeholders in conjunction with relevant government agencies must constitute assessment teams who should be saddled with specific timeframe monitoring activities and filing in relevant reports to enhance situational intervention. These teams should be saddled with responsibility to conduct programming assessment on community returnees to determine the effectiveness of their community-based transitional programs, which they are enrolled in. The time-to-time monitoring schedule should be a continuum for minimum of 2 years to ensure these individuals properly adjust to community life.

(10)   In a world where offenders are gaining the momentum to force the arms of government for advance and additional cares. The victims of crime, who have gotten everything to lose, must not be abandoned to their travail and suffering: mentally, socially, relationship-wise and/or materially. They deserve better than what those who victimized them could get.

13.1 The 11th Recommendation with A Subtitle: "De-Institutionalization of The Current System of Imprisonment (Offenders' Treatment) Within the Capitalist Economy of The United States – A Reform Panacea"

Preamble: According to The Sentencing Project's (2021) statistical facts: "There are (approximately) **2 million** people in the (USA) nation's prisons and jails—a 500% increase over the last 40 years. Changes in sentencing law and policy, not changes in crime rates, explain most of this increase." *Roy (2018) and Kang-Brown et al., (2021)* shared the same view, stating: "while the United States represents about 4.2 percent of the world's population, it houses around 20 percent (20%) of the world's prisoners." "Corrections (which includes prisons, jails, probation, and parole) cost around $74 billion in 2007 according to the U.S. Bureau of Justice Statistics (2011)." Further on *Justice Expenditures and Employment in the United States, 2017* report release by BJS, (the report) estimated that county and municipal governments spent roughly US$30 billion on corrections in 2017 (Bureau of Justice Statistics, 2021).

The essence of the 11th Recommendation is to elaborate the submission of the 2nd Recommendation that "there is a need to explore alternative to incarceration in 21st century America. Since the overwhelming analysis on the effect of incarceration has built towards how offenders in US have come to accept the prison life as a new world to build their own socialization and subculture to avoid the innate ability to be responsible for themselves in the capitalist world. The acceptance of Prison life is directly influencing the increasing figures of prisoners and, the push to identify as offenders with mental illness issues. National Institute of Justice corroborated this fact as reported by World Population Review thus: '…almost 44% of criminals released return before the end of their first year out of prison. In 2005, about 68% of 405,000 prisoners that were released were arrested for a new crime within three years, and 77% were arrested within five years.' The number of people who will reengage with the criminal justice system highlights the critical importance (…) (Martin and Garcia, 2022)."

According to Vera Institute which also shares the submission of this research recommendation and the objective to put a stop to continue human rusting in jails rather than allowing these individuals to be positively engaged in profitable ventures during their existence. The Non-governmental body further louds this in its mission statement, stating that its mission is to end overcriminalization and mass incarceration of immigrants and ordinary people experiencing poverty. Or those who only need some moral upgrade but are rather perpetually locked up, wasting away with all naturally given endowments. Jennifer Vollen Katz, the Media Executive Director of John Howard Association stated in her submission: "…based on what we hear, see, learn and observed during our monitoring visits; JHA believes proper treatment management of (these prisoners) should be done in a more (de-institutionalized setting), not in a prison."

To further buttress the above, a renown mental health practitioner who preferred to being quoted anonymously stated: "as a mental health professional with about 20 years in-service experience, I clearly believe this will be good option for the government and for everyone, rather than continuing to invest in employing tons of Psychiatrist-professionals to place these young incarcerated persons on strength-extracting medications and trapping them down with therapeutic chains every day. Such strength we are caging and trapping down can be positively unleashed in productive ventures, I will submit."

The Economic Boosting Potency of this reform Initiative carefully analyzes the "De-institutionalization" process of the current method of US imprisonment and offenders' treatment system so as to:

(i)   Not only assist in halting the chain of overwhelmingly increasing number of offenders who continue to criminogenically create episodes of mental illness to get in line and increase the queue of offenders on the waiting list for institutional treatment, but to be able to stop the continuous on-towards expenditure pressure on government resources and indeed tax-payers' fund.

(ii)   To be able to build economic prospects out of the proposed treatment rearrangement rather than continuing to allow offenders to manipulate the system and create self-benefitting loops in Criminal Justice process after committing crime and at the same time draining economic resources meant for socioeconomic development for the rest populace. And third,

(iii)   To be able to effectively address the recidivists' chain: save the cost of offenders' re-arrest, the cost of rearraignment and the cost of reincarceration of same offenders over and over again as documented in several research findings. But rather, to progressively fulfill the two main ideological goals which incarceration should be addressing in 21st century competitive economies. These include: (a) de-institutionalization of offenders' treatment for increased social safety and (b) for commerce-driven economy of scale. (See recommendations of MD Pablo's Federal Monitor Report's recommendation like other previously submitted research papers which suggest de-institutionalization of offenders' treatment). To enhance and achieve the commerce-driven approach in de-institutionalized treatment setting, the policy measures include:

(i)   Unlocking the natural ability of the incarcerated young men and women whose youthful strength should be contributory to the economy and the future development of America rather than locking down millions of (such) non-dangerous young individuals' vigor within the 4-wall of prison and stressing out the rest population to fend for their needs.

Hence, the strategy of de-institutionalization treatment in deploying youthful offenders to revamp commence in rural agriculture, mining and other exploration sectors through secured deployment and self-contributory individualized wellness treatment.

(ii) Identifying the right approach to human wellness in line with research recommendations in sustainable health and wellness. Since, many unhealthy mental episodes of many incarcerated individuals build up overtime within their duration of incarceration which suggest strong correlation between passive utilization of youthful vigor and mental dysfunction. Hence, the need to resolve this wellness complication for individuals in custody by actively engaging them in viable production sectors while serving their terms. More so, since active engagement of human-body composition is often the best therapeutic treatment for both mental and physical wellness. Remember, the core approach to mental health treatment revolves largely around therapeutic treatment.

(iii) Shooting for full de-institutionalized programs of incarcerated offenders by calling for pre-qualification and licensure of new privately owned (Corporations) and privately managed commerce-related security subsidiary companies who will employed and train new personnel as 'warders' and securely engaged offenders as commercialized entities, including managing such offenders' individualized treatment plans.

(iv) Saddling these business entities with responsibilities to utilize their trained personnel to lead non-violent offenders to daily deployment and back to their secured base. While the new qualified private companies are expected to be upshoot or subsidiaries of established corporations with existing sites where offenders can be securely managed within close proximity-setting to their daily deployment or work sites. Where such new subsidiary companies shall also receive designated numbers of working offenders based on the companies' assessed managerial security capacity.

(v)   Liberalization of licensing for subsidiary companies to recruit their own health workers and specialists based on the need of their serving population of incarcerated offenders.

(vi)   Deployment of Department of Correction employees to work with new subsidiary companies to create ideal work-hour charts, programming and rehabilitation templates as well as other legal prerequired logs for proper accountability of offenders' activities.

(vii)   Liberalization of licensing for subsidiary companies to be able to employ their own servicing companies in food supplies and other technical maintenance.

(viii) Have all department(s) of correction (in USA) function ONLY as government regulatory agencies aside retaining violent offenders within the traditional prison custody.

The above initiative is no doubt aiming towards massive employment generation as well as formation of new subsidiary companies. And to address the issue of broader impact of this initiative, no doubt, the initiative will without doubt put the United States at a vantage position to be able to explore previous areas of economic production challenges, which improved productivity can enhance massive exportation in key agricultural, mining and in oil exploration sectors to mention just a few. Other economic and security viabilities of this initiative include:

(i)   Improved economic of scale for the capitalist economy of the United States in international competitiveness.

(ii)   Reduction in diversion of tax-payers' fund which is utilized in servicing uneconomical cost of imprisonment.

(iii) Refocusing of government expenditure to public amenities and infrastructural improvement aside social institutions' rehabilitation and reconstruction, such as: new schools and health care centers.

(iv)   This initiative will also guarantee massive reduction in the number of incarcerated offenders within the first 2 years of its implementation. By so doing, resolving a major concern for the government of the United States. The above result will be achieved as a direct result of bringing an end to lazy lifestyle which current traditional mode of incarceration encouraged. And by so doing, discouraging prisoners who have accepted imprisonment as a life-venture and as well as a hiding place to lazy-around rather than standing up to fend for themselves in a capitalist economy. This initiative will also stop millions of youths getting mentally crippled by the lazy-life embedded in traditional imprisonment.

(v)   The initiative will equally help many released offenders survive faster after years of incarceration. The work-ethic, which these prisoners will imbibe in the course of implementation of this new reform-initiative, will position them more advantageously after their prison terms.

Law-Makers and other governmental apparatus in both Federal and States are enjoined to utilize their legislative positions and policy enactment-authority to advance the execution prospect of this carefully researched commerce enhancing de-institutionalization treatment initiative so as to be able to reap its economic multiplier effects as well as the global replicability of the ideological reform. Putting America first for bringing about this needed reform-revolution in offenders' treatment and imprisonment practice.

Again, by achieving the above, the United States will automatically become the leading government in championing the 21st century commerce-driven reformation of offenders' treatment through de-institutionalization. Especially more as an initiative geared towards guaranteeing a safer society, zero-rate of recidivism, expenditure preservation and massive job creativity chiefly after a covid-19 burdened economy.

References

Alper, M., Durose, M.R. & Markman, J. (*2018*). *Update on Prisoner Recidivism: A 9-Year Follow-up Period (2005-2014)* (pdf, 31 pages), Bureau of Justice Statistics Special Report, May 2018, NCJ 250975.

American Civil Liberties Union (2022) America's Addiction to Juvenile Incarceration: State by State | American Civil Liberties Union (aclu.org)https://www.aclu.org › issues › youthincarceration › ame... viewed: 3/29/2022

Benecchi, L. (2021). Recidivism Imprisons American Progress. Source: https://harvardpolitics.com/recidivism-americanprogress/ viewed: 4/22/2022.

Bible society (2021 ed.) "What causes mental Illness: etiology & Bible" source: https://www.bible.ca/psychiatry/psychiatrymental-illness-causes-etiology.htm viewed: 4/5/2022

Bureau of Justice Statistics. *Prison and Jail Inmates at Midyear* series for 1998, 1999, 2002, 2003, & 2004; *Jail Inmates at Midyear 2014*, and the *Jail Inmates* series for 2015-2018. Available from: https://www.bjs.gov/. viewed: 3/29/2022

Bureau of Justice Statistics (2021). "Justice Expenditures and Employment in the United States, 2017". U.S. Department of Justice; Office of Justice Programs; Bureau of Justice Statistics. July 2021.

Bureau of Justice Statistics (2020) - Prison population counts. https://www.bjs.gov/. viewed: 3/29/2022

Cloyes KG, Wong B, &Latimer S, (2010). Time to prison return for offenders with serious mental illness released from prison. A survival analysis. Criminal Justice Behavior, 2010 Feb;37(2):175-87.

Criminal Lawyer Group (2021) 'The evolution of criminal justice" source: https://www.criminallawyergroup.com/theevolution-of-criminal-justice/ viewed: 3/31/2022)

Dalgleish, D. (2005). *"Pre-Colonial Criminal Justice in West Africa: Eurocentric Thought Versus Africentric Evidence" (PDF)*. African Journal of Criminology and Justice Studies. 1 (1). *Retrieved 2011-06-26*.

Dehert, M. (2018). 'Physical illness in patients with severe mental disorders' World Psychiatry 2011: volume 10, issue 1, pages 52 to 77.

Dempsey, J. S.; and Forst, L. S. (2015). An Introduction to Policing (8 ed.). Cengage Learning. pp. 6–8. ISBN 978-1305544680.

Eck, W. and Takács, S. A. (2003). The Age of Augustus. Translated by Schneider, Deborah Lucas. Oxford: Blackwell. p. 79. ISBN 0-631-22957-4.

Federal Bureau of Prison (2018) BOP Statistics: Average Inmate Age. Internet citation: *OJJDP Statistical Briefing*

Book. Online. Source: https://www.ojjdp.gov/ojstatbb/corrections/qa08700.asp?qaDate=2018. viewed: 3/29/2022

First Annual Report of Monitor Pablo Stewart, MD on Ashoor Rasho et al., Plaintiffs, vs Director John R. Baldwin, et al., Defendants 2017

Heller T (1997). 'Benefits of support groups for families of adults with severe mental illness' American Journal of Orthopsychiatry 1997: volume 67, issue 2, pages 187 to 198.

Herman, C. (2018). News Report: "Court Monitor 'Absolutely Convinced' Mentally Ill Inmates Abused, Inadequately Treated In Illinois" Source: The Appeal, 2018: Court Monitor 'Absolutely Convinced' Mentally Ill Inmates Abused, Inadequately Treated In Illinois | Illinois Public Media News | Illinois Public Media. Viewed: 04/09/2022.

Human Rights Watch (2012). Ill-equipped: U.S. prisons and offenders with mental illness. Source: http://www.hrw.org/en/reports/2003/10/2 1/ill-equipped. Viewed: 4/12/2022.

Hunter, V. J. (1994). Policing Athens: Social Control in the Attic Lawsuits, 420–320 B.C. Princeton, New Jersey: Princeton University Press. p. 3. ISBN 978-069-165689-2. Archived from the original on 2007-0421.

Ill. Admin. Code: *Amended at 27 Ill. Reg. 6214, effective May 01, 2003*

Ill. Admin. Code tit. 20 § 504.12: Amended at 41 Ill. Reg. 3869, effective April 1, 2017 Illinois Administrative Code | Subpart A - ADMINISTRATION OF DISCIPLINE | Casetext viewed: 4/4/2022)

Ill. Admin. Code: Amended at 41 Ill. Reg. 3869, effective 4/1/2017 (Section 504.810 - Filing of Grievances, Ill. Admin. Code tit. 20 § 504.810 | Case text Search + Citator viewed: 4/4/2022)

Kang-Brown, Jacob; Montagnet, Chase and Heiss, Jasmine (2021). "People in Jail and Prison in 2020." Source: https://en.wikipedia.org/wiki/United_States_incarceration_rate. Viewed: 5/28/2022.

Knapp, M., Beecham, J., McDaid, D., Matosevic, T., Smith, M. (2011). The economic consequences of deinstitutionalization of mental health services: lessons from a systematic review of European experience. *Health and Social Care in the Community,* 19(2): 113-125.

Lamb, H.R., Weinberger, L.E. (2005). The shift of psychiatric inpatient care from hospitals to jails and prisons. *J Am Acad Psychiatry Law,* 33: 529-34.

Langeluttig, A.(1927). The Department of Justice of the United States. Johns Hopkins Press. pp. 14–15.

Latarski, S. (2020). "Recidivism in the United States – An Overview" Source: https://atlascorps.org/recidivism-united-statesoverview/ viewed: 4/22/2022

Lovell D, Gagliardi G.J., & Peterson P.D. (2002). Recidivism and use of services among persons with mental illness after release from prison. Psychiatric Services 2002 Oct;53(10):1290-6. PMID: 12364677

Martin, E. &Garcia, M (2022) "Robust Evidence for High-Stakes Decision-Making" National Institute of Justice Journal. Source: ttps://nij.ojp.gov/topics/articles/

reentry-researchnij-providing-robust-evidence-high-stakes-decisionmaking.Viewed: 4/22/2022.

Martinez-Leal, R., et. al. (2011). The impact of living arrangements and deinstitutionalization in the health status of persons with intellectual disability in Europe. *J Intellect Disability Res*, 55(9): 858-872.

McKean, L. and Ransford, C. (2004). "Current Strategies for Reducing Recidivism." Center for Impact Research Reports. Source: Microsoft Word - Recidivism final cover. doc (issuelab.org). Viewed: 4/22/2022

McPhillips, D. (2016). U.S. Among Most Depressed Countries in the World National Alliance of Mental Health reports.

Mental Health America (2020) "What causes mental illness?" Source: https://screening.mhanational.org/content/whatcauses-mental-illness/ viewed: 4/21/2022

Murthy, R. S. et al. (2002). The World Health Report 2001: Mental Health, New Understanding, New Hope (Reprint ed.). Geneva: World Health Organization. ISBN 9789241562010.

National Institute of Justice, "2021 Review and Revalidation of the First Step Act Risk Assessment Tool," Washington, DC: U.S. Department of Justice, National Institute of Justice, December 2021.

National Institute of Justice (2018). "Measuring Recidivism." Source: https://nij.ojp.gov/topics/articles/measuringrecidivism. Viewed: 4/22/2022

NCBI (2021) Sources: https:// www.ncbi.nlm.nih.gov/pmc/articles/PMC2811042/. Viewed: 10/14/2021

Novella, E.J. (2010). Mental health care and the politics of inclusion: a social systems account of psychiatric deinstitutionalization. *Theor Med Bioeth*, 31: 411-427.

Reginal Criminal Defence Lawyers (2022). The history of the criminal justice system and its evaluation time to time. Source: https://criminallawyerregina.ca/brief-history-ofcriminal-justice-system/. Viewed: 3/31/2022

Roy, Walmsley (2018), "World Prison Population List, 12th edition (12th ed.)." Source: https://en.wikipedia.org/wiki/United_States_incarc eration_rate. Viewed: 5/28/2022

Bureau of Justice Statistics (2011). "Justice Expenditures and Employment, FY 1982-2007 - Statistical Tables." Source: https://en.wikipedia.org/wiki/United_States_incarc eration_rate. Viewed: 5/28/2022.

Sirotich F. (2009). The criminal justice outcomes of jail diversion programs for persons with mental illness: a review of the evidence. J Am Acad Psychiatry Law 2009 Dec;37(4):461-72. PMID: 20018995

Terrill, R. J. (2015). World Criminal Justice Systems: A Comparative Survey (revised ed.). Routledge. p. 32. ISBN 978-1317228820.

The Sentencing Project (2021). "FACT SHEET: TRENDS IN U.S. CORRECTIONS." Source: https://www.sentencingproject.org/wpcontent/uploads/2021/07/Trends-in-USCorrections.pdf. Viewed: 5/27/2022.

Wang, P.S. (2010). "Rethinking mental illness". JAMA. 303 (19): 1970– 1971. doi:10.1001/jama.2010.555. PMID 20483974.S2CID 8210144.

Weill-Greenberg, E. (2018). 'No Shower, Wearing Diapers, Laying There for So Long' - The Appeal, 2018. Source: "https://theappeal.org/no-shower-wearingdiapers-laying-there-for-so-long/" viewed: 04/12/2022

World Health Organization (2001). The World Health Report 2001 – Mental health: new understanding new hope. Source: http://www.who.int/mental_health/en/. Viewed: 4/07/2022

World Population Review "Recidivism" Source: ttps://www.yardtimeent.org/thefacts#:~:text=Recidivism%20In%20America&text=A ccording%20to%20the%20National%20Institute,we re%20arrested%20within%20five%20years. Viewed: 4/21/2022.

Worthy, L. D; Lavigne, T, and Romero, F (2020) "Culture and Psychology: The History of Mental Illness" Maricopa: Mmoer. Source: Culture and Psychology – Simple Book Publishing (maricopa.edu) viewed: 4/5/2022

730 ILCS 5/Ch. VIII Art. 6 heading ARTICLE 6. EFFECTIVE DATE (730 ILCS 5/8-6-1) (from Ch. 38, par. 1008-6-1) Sec. 8-6-1. Effective Date: Jan. 1, 1973. Source: P.A. 77-2097.)